YOUR ENGLISH
is better than
MY FRENCH

ADVENTURES IN FRANCE AND
HACKS FOR A GREAT VACATION

ERIC KIRCHMANN

ISBN: 979-8-9874945-0-9 (paperback)
ISBN: 979-8-9874945-1-6 (ebook)

Library of Congress Control Number: 2022923831

Editors: Susan Keillor, Connie Kirchmann
Book Design and Layout: Jose Pepito Jr.

For Courtney and the wonderful people of France

CONTENTS

PREFACE

A s empty nesters finally able to travel extensively, looking forward to and planning our next big trip is one of our greatest joys. Courtney and I were bitten by the travel bug on our trip to France in 2014. My book, *Écoutez et Répétez*, was a love letter to Courtney documenting the trip with words and pictures to cherish forever. Exploring the world together, travel became our happy place. This love was amplified by an extraordinary trip to Italy in 2018, which yielded my second book, *And All I Got Was Cheese...* Now with money set aside, it was time to plan our next trip. We debated locations but settled on returning to France in large part to finally see Paris. Going back to junior high French class together, this had always been our dream. We avoided it on our first European trip because we wanted to figure out international travel and better understand the culture before attempting to crack the magnetic but intimidating city. As detailed in *Écoutez et Répétez*, we made a ton of mistakes on that first trip but also learned so much. Now, we felt ready for Paris. Unfortunately, this was the trip that was never going to happen...

In the spring of 2019, we began to research and plan for a May 2020 vacation. All through the rest of 2019, we reserved fantastic looking rental places, booked our plane reservations, and even reserved tickets for various tourist sites. In all, we pre-paid thousands of dollars. We researched restaurants, boulangeries, patisseries, and had even put together our itinerary. Our plan was to spend a week in Paris, followed by several days in the Loire Valley, finishing up with a week in the Dordogne. We studied the language, re-learning our French. After many years of French in school and refreshing it prior to our 2014 trip, it came back quickly. As the year turned to 2020, our excitement grew.

When I first heard of the COVID-19 outbreak in China, I wasn't overly concerned. It seemed remote, and Asia had previously endured other emerging viruses without spreading to the rest of the world. Then it hit New York, and the rest of the country went into a preventive "temporary" lockdown. I remember thinking it would only last a couple months and be gone in time for our trip. When American sports leagues shut down, and the nation (and entire world) ground to a complete halt, it dawned on us that our trip was not happening. Excitement for the trip morphed into grave concern for my parents with preexisting conditions and our daughter, Kelsey, pregnant with our first grandchild. We kept both in complete isolation, resorting to Zoom calls for family interactions. Feeling sick in the pit of my stomach, I worked at cancelling our trip. Remarkably, all of the pre-paid money (except for thirty dollars) was refunded.

We all have our pandemic stories to tell. In the end, we feel quite lucky; no one got sick. I was fortunate to be able to perform most of my job from home via telehealth. I did spend a couple anxious weekends on-call to the hospital working in space-suit-like protective gear. But compared to others, we fared pretty well. Since we couldn't travel out of the country, we found an inexpensive long term beach rental, and I worked remote from the beach during October 2020 (and May 2021). Despite this luxury, we still fell prey to social isolation and COVID-induced anxiety and depression.

The silver lining in our COVID cloud was the birth of our precious granddaughter, Cora, in November 2020. Both families remained in strict isolation to protect Cora as the respective grandmothers split childcare duties while Kelsey and her husband, David, worked remote. Cora brought a previously unimaginable joy to our lives. Still working remote myself, I was able to spend infinitely more time with her than I could have if I had been working in person.

After the winter wave of COVID passed, I kept my eyes on travel restrictions, hoping the worst was over and wishfully thinking a 2021 spring trip might yet be possible. During the lull, we started to tentatively plan again. Courtney talked me out of the Loire, and we planned instead more time in Paris and added a few days in Gascony, home of my favorite liquor, Armagnac. We planned just enough to get excited again, but travel restrictions were NOT lifted as France remained one of the countries most ravaged by the virus. The Delta variant caused us to cancel a smaller trip to New Orleans we had hopefully planned with friends for October. Pandemic fatigue and depression hit hard. I actually found it painful to think of our trip to France, which seemed would never happen.

Studying the rise and fall of variant peaks, we planned yet another trip, this time with my parents, to visit Barbados in December. Numbers were falling in America. However, as we approached the trip, Delta infections skyrocketed in Barbados. We cancelled that trip too, this time losing much of the money. We were able to spend a few rejuvenating days in San Diego instead. As Delta continued to wane in America and Europe, we began to plan for France in 2022. We again started to reserve places to stay and bought plane tickets. This trip was happening come hell or high water… I hoped. Hope was dashed again when the Omicron variant hit. Despite the latest wave, I kept planning but had a heavy feeling in my gut that told me the trip might not ever happen.

The prospects of the trip became a roller coaster. As Omicron began to wane in late winter, the trip appeared a very real possibility. Shortly thereafter, Russia invaded Ukraine, throwing all of Europe into chaos. Travel to France now seemed like an iffy proposition. Then, Omicron B hit France, and with rates rising, we held our breath, fearing travel restrictions would be reimposed. Miraculously, six weeks before the trip, the infection rate came down steadily in France. Our excitement building, we thought we might make the trip yet. We began to make actual restaurant reservations and final preparations. Two weeks out, Omicron B hit North Carolina, causing us to go back into strict isolation to avoid infection. Twelve days out, we started to shift our bedtime with our melatonin schedule. We finalized our packing lists. Before we knew it, the trip that was never going to happen was here.

The "never to be" trip ended up being a truly remarkable and fabulous journey. We learned from our mistakes during our first French trip and picked up a lot of new tricks along the way. With rare exception, we found the people of France uniformly wonderful and welcoming. Reflecting on the trip, we still can't believe how we managed to pack in so many phenomenal experiences during the three weeks. What follows is, first, a compilation of all we have learned about how to navigate French culture, which is then followed by our tale, one adventure after another. Enjoy!

FRENCH HACKS FOR A GREAT VACATION

S ome of you may remember my first book, *Écoutez et Répétez*, detailing our trip to France in 2014. Despite having worked to learn about language, culture, and etiquette, we always seemed to be atop the European Faux Pas Leader Board. No matter how hard we tried, we were always doing something wrong. With our very average language skills and the expectation of the French that we should know the correct way to do things without being told, we often weren't even sure what we did wrong. While few seemed ready to help us get it right, many were quick to let us know, in no uncertain terms, that we got it wrong! Even with our missteps, we still had a spectacular first trip to France which made us want to go back again and again.

This time, in preparation, we devoured endless blogs, videos and books on culture, etiquette, clothing, language, restaurants and especially cafés! Much of it was quite helpful, but a lot of it was completely off. Obviously, the best way to learn is by being there and living it. As we learned, we started writing down a running list of "hacks" for getting along well in France. As I said in the preface, we were delighted (and a little surprised in Paris) with the, almost, uniformly lovely reception we received from the French people. That being said, we observed many instances of Americans not having a good time. We do not at all claim to be experts, but hope this list may assist others (and remind ourselves for next time) with hints that can make the experience better. What follows is a comprehensive list of hacks in categories. **If you are not planning a trip to France, feel free to skip to the next chapter, where our voyage begins.**

A. Language Preparation

This is quite possibly the most important thing I can emphasize. Your ability to have genuinely warm interactions with the French is greatly improved with some language skills. You may be thinking, "I've never learned any French," and feel this task is daunting, but the truth is you don't need to be fluent or even that proficient to be successful. In France, you just have to try. Courtney and I took five years of French together, then over the next twenty-five years forgot it all and have now tried to re-learn it three times. My natural talent for language is nil, but I am persistent. I usually spend about eight months or more working on language before I travel. At the end of each trip, I am always glad I did. Courtney has a natural talent for language and especially for correct pronunciation, but she prefers the cramming method in the last couple months. Both approaches have worked. So how do we suggest you go about it?

You can pay a lot of money for courses and online sites if you wish. Being fairly cheap, I like to use mostly free methods. We have had a **Rosetta Stone** subscription for many years. It was fairly pricey. This method works for me, but Courtney finds it repetitive and monotonous

(I am not sure what that says about my personality). We both like the **Duolingo** app, which can be used for free and moves you along quicker. You can test out of easy skills, and it is engaging like a video game. If you ask me, the paid version of the site doesn't add much other than unlimited "hearts" (akin to lives in a video game) and isn't worth it unless you are in cram mode. Another favorite of mine is the *Coffee Break French* podcast series. I think there are now eleven seasons, starting from the very basics and moving forward to more conversational seasons. The host is engaging and provides easy-to-understand explanations, which often include useful cultural references and etiquette tips. As the name suggests, each podcast lasts about fifteen to thirty minutes and were perfect for my commute. There is also a paid version which adds additional resources, and may be worth it, but I've never sprung for it. The *Coffee Break* series is available for many other languages as well, and I highly recommend it.

There are other ways to immerse yourself in the language. One thing we do for several months ahead of a trip is watch TV programming in the local language with English subtitles. A word of caution—don't let this overwhelm you when you initially can't pick out a single word. The more you watch, though, the more you eventually pick up. Some series are delivered in very complex, rapid-fire French, but others are much easier to understand. Some of our favorites are *Spiral, A French Village, Call My Agent, Lupin, Le Chalet, The Bonfire of Destiny* and *The Returned*. (The same two French stars showed up in almost every series, Thierry Goddard and Audrey Fleurot. It became our running joke to express faux shock when they appeared in each new show we watched.)

I am a big fan of **Google Maps**. Another thing you can do months in advance is change your guiding voice to French and your distances to metric. This teaches you driving terms and gets you used to kilometer distances, both of which help when you are driving helter-skelter in France. Also, start thinking in terms of the twenty-four-hour clock.

B. Trip Planning

I know this is not a big surprise, but I am detail oriented. Starting early and being very organized makes a big difference for European vacations. Courtney found an app called **Bublup** that we used for the first time. This allowed both of us to add to trip planning at the shared site, which we could then access on the trip without the need for paper copies. I am sure there are other apps out there, but this one worked well for us.

<u>Season</u>

We read a lot of differing opinions on the best time to visit, Paris in particular. Being empty nesters, we settled on late May. Hitting it just as travel was opening up after the pandemic surely helped, but we didn't experience the hordes of tourists you read about during the summer months. Paris was beautiful in May, and much was in bloom. Parisian weather can vary widely. We had several steamy hot days but also cold, rainy ones. A jacket or heavy windbreaker was needed many nights in Paris. I imagine April is cooler yet. If you are going during summer months, expect more crowds and make sure your accommodations have air conditioning (most places in Paris do not). None of the three places we stayed across France had A/C and would have been uncomfortable in heavier heat. They say August is when all Parisians leave on holiday, and the city is populated mainly by tourists. It may not be the best month if you are looking for authentic. We were happy with our choice of May, and I imagine the fall shoulder season would be a great time to visit as well.

<u>Guidebooks</u>

I wouldn't invest a ton of money on guidebooks which mostly give an overview. If they are a year or two old, you can find much more current info online. If you do buy a guidebook, I suggest the **Michelin Green Guides** for France. There are books for most regions, and while they are not the end all, be all, they do provide basic background information and useful maps. We structured a lot of our walks and scenic drives around those found in the Green Guides.

Research, Research, Research

You can stay in hotels if you want the assurance of a name brand or a foolproof reservation, but you will pay a lot more. In Europe, we have always stayed in an **Airbnb**, **VRBO** or a bed-and-breakfast. First, figure out what neighborhoods or regions you would like to target and then sort them by the price you are willing to pay and number of reviews (I never trust anything with zero or only a few reviews). Then, read the reviews obsessively. If you are persistent, you will find some amazingly great places with accommodating hosts and stellar reviews. We have had a couple stays which did not live up to our lofty expectations, but most have been all that and more. For example, all three places we stayed this time would have slept four, came equipped with full kitchens (which saves lots of money), and were in great locations. Paris cost us about $180 per night, taxes included, and both places in the southwest of France cost around $100-125 per night, taxes also included. Unbelievable!

Next start researching restaurants, boulangeries/patisseries, and dessert places. I love **TripAdvisor** and also use **Google** reviews. Our plan is usually to splurge on a really nice restaurant once or twice, but we otherwise look for "hidden gems." We specifically look for mid-priced places where reviews rave about the staff, the food, and share pictures that look delectable. Try your best to stay away from tourist traps, which typically ring all the major attractions. You are looking for authentic mom and pop joints in real neighborhoods. A dead give-away are places with, say, seventy-five glowing reviews in French (most French do not "glow" in their reviews) and only two in English. Use

Google Translate to read the French reviews. For each neighborhood (in Paris, "arrondissement"), try to target three or four great looking restaurants and a couple dessert/ice cream/pastry places. This ends up being overkill given you cannot possibly visit all of them. However, in Paris, your agenda timeline easily gets warped, and you often aren't where you thought you'd be at mealtime. This way, you always have a few good options close by.

<u>Agenda</u>

Start talking early about what attractions you want to focus on. Paris has more to do than you could possibly accomplish in multiple vacations. Do not try to do too much (my fatal flaw), just plan to come back! As you sketch out your agenda, pay close attention to what days each place is closed. Everything in all of France is closed at least two days a week, but not everything is closed on the same days. Sunday and Monday are big days for closings, so start by planning these two days first with places which are open, then work around them. A picnic in one of Paris' incredible parks is a good option for one of these days. Three other items to consider: First, market days in France are awesome. However, each market is fully open only on certain days. Try to plan some of your time around open markets (market tips below). Second, do NOT plan to get anything done between say 11:45am and 2pm. Most shops and some attractions are closed for the traditional two-hour French lunch. Don't be frustrated by this. Instead, find a table, sit down, and savor every minute of it. Finally, be flexible with your agenda. Stuff happens—some things take longer than planned, you might tire out and decide to sit down for a glass of wine instead, and you WILL get lost (a joy in Paris because you almost always run into something amazing and unexpected while lost). On the flexibility topic, depending on the length of your trip, leave the last day or two as "flex" days to either fit in places you missed earlier or for activities you didn't realize you really wanted to do until you got on the ground. Or maybe just spend the flex time wandering ("flaneur" in French) and soak up the atmosphere.

Make Reservations Ahead of Time

Most big attractions (the Louvre, Musée d'Orsay, Sainte-Chapelle and the like) have online, timed tickets you can buy months in advance. For busy attractions, choose the earliest visiting times to avoid crowds. Alternatively, some attractions clear out in the evening, making later visits work well. This avoids a lot of standing in line. For great restaurants you don't want to miss, advanced reservations are a must. Don't make reservations for every meal, but do get several to have in hand. Some restaurants have online reservations, many of them through **The Fork** app, which is a relief. However, many of the "hidden gems" require you to call directly…

If you are like me, your anxiety goes through the roof at the thought of attempting your first real French conversation over the phone making reservations. Relax, though. You may screw up the first one or two, but you will get the hang of it. I find making international calls through wi-fi with **Skype** one of the easiest ways. Set up an account, deposit ten bucks, and you can call for a few cents a minute. Write out your French script, practice it, and have it at the ready. Think about France being six hours ahead. They will be more patient if you are not calling during their busy time. I found calling over our lunch hour, which is 6-7pm in France, a good time to call. They are usually present to answer, but the dinner crowd is still at least an hour away. When answered, dive in with:

> "Bonsoir, Monsieur (or Madame)" *[Use bonjour if it is earlier than 6pm there.]* "Je voudrais faire une reservation pour une table pour deux, le huit Juin à vingt heures." [I would like to make a reservation for a table for two, June eighth at twenty hundred hours]

If they don't understand you, they will often break into English to help you. The less brave way to do this is to start with, "Parlez-vous anglais?" [Do you speak English?] which may or may not get you decent service. Thinking about dinner reservations, don't make them before 8pm in Paris as it will mark you as a tourist, and they may laugh and tell you, "Ce n'est pas possible." [It is not possible.] A favorite phrase of the French, especially when talking to foreigners. In rural parts of France, they do tend to eat a little earlier, but not much.

C. Clothing/Packing

Clothing

This is one of the biggest areas of misinformation on the internet. Blogs will insist: "Wear this, not that," and "Absolutely do not ever think of wearing that!" Our first time in France, we were very self-conscious about our wardrobe. Giving off this vibe shows through and is not re-spected by the French. What we learned in Paris this time is that you can wear just about anything you want, within reason, as long as you wear it with confidence. In the end, nobody really cares. Now don't get me wrong, if you wear cargo shorts, old tennis shoes, and a 'Merica t-shirt, you will certainly get some glares. In our opinion, it is best to blend in with classy, basic elements which can be combined into many different looks. While blending in, do not try too hard. Unless you are a man who usually sports man scarfs, avoid trying to pull this off. Also, almost everyone wearing a beret is a tourist until proven otherwise.

For women, Courtney recommends neutral colors, high quality denim (jackets and pants), upscale tailoring, and eyelet shirts for sum-mer. Anything from Madewell would work at the time of this writing. Interesting belts and scarves top off the look. Dainty, subtle jewelry is in. A little black dress that you can dress up or down covers most fancy dinners. Above all, for both men and women, comfortable, broken-in shoes are a must; miles on Paris cobblestones make anything else untenable. Flats or espadrilles are good choices. Fashionable sneakers are very acceptable.

For men, I recommend lots of lightweight Merino wool shirts which are cooling, never wrinkle, and dry overnight even if you only have a sink to work with. Parisians love their jeans, especially Levi's hilariously. Otherwise, I wore tan slacks mostly of the no-wrinkle, traveler variety. I chose not to wear any shorts in Paris, but I could have without any problem. A couple of nice collared shirts with slacks work for most restaurants. I took a traveler's sports jacket, which was appreciated at one very fancy restaurant, but it was the only time I wore it. I wore nice quality leather chukka boots and comfortable but stylish loafers. I didn't take sneakers, but I could have if they were new, subtle, and of high quality.

Packing

Okay, here's our best advice after three big trips. Make a list of how many items of clothing you would usually haul in your SUV on an American vacation and then cross off about two-thirds of them. You will be dragging suitcases on cobblestones, trying to protect them on the Métro, and carrying them up many flights of stairs in buildings without lifts. After every trip, we say we wish we had taken less (it leaves more room for souvenirs too). This trip we actually did better. One thing I did underestimate was socks and underwear. After walking all day in the heat then getting ready for dinner at night, a few extra pairs are useful and don't take up much space. We traveled with two medium sized suitcases, which we checked, two backpacks, and a larger carry-on backpack that attached to a suitcase when rolling. As a side note, making sure your rentals have a washer helps tremendously in packing light.

D. Phase Shifting Your Sleep Schedule ────────────

Jet lag sucks, especially if it ruins your first two days. Many years ago, I found a small study in the medical literature for beating jet lag and have adapted it over the years. Basically, over about ten days, you gradually move your bedtime here toward your preferred bedtime at your new location, one half-hour at a time, tricking your brain with melatonin. At the end, you end up going to bed pretty much right after work and getting up super early in the morning. It feels a little weird but is worth it. At bedtimes when it is still light out, use a sleep mask or blackout curtains. When waking up in the dark, turn on all the lights in the house and try to be active. If you can book a flight leaving in the evening around 6pm (midnight in Paris), take your sleep medication when you board the flight and wake up on landing ready to go. Do not nap on the first day and continue to take melatonin at your preferred bedtime for a few more days. In the mornings, get out in the sunshine right away. You can usually get quite a bit done the first day even if you feel a little bit sluggish, but by day two, you already feel great. We don't reverse shift at the end of the trip because we want to enjoy every minute. You pay for it on your return, but who cares? Sample protocol:

T-10 days	11pm bedtime	5mg melatonin (I take 10mg myself as an insomniac)
T-9	10:30pm	5mg
T-8	10pm	5mg
T-7	9:30pm	5mg
T-6	9pm	5mg
T-5	8:30pm	5mg
T-4	8pm	5mg
T-3	7:30pm	5mg
T-2	7pm	5mg
T-1	6:30pm	5mg
Flight day	6pm if possible	5mg

E. The Proper Politeness

I could easily make the case this may be even more important than language preparation. In every shop, market, restaurant, and café, start EVERY conversation with "Bonjour Monsieur!" (or Madame). Say it in a respectful and cheerful way as you enter through the door. Try to say it first. All is lost if they have to greet you! If it is past about 6pm, say "Bonsoir." This is very much expected, and if you do not show this common courtesy, you are already behind. If the shop owner is occupied in conversation, don't interrupt with your greeting but instead make eye contact, nod, and maybe whisper or mouth bonjour. When you leave any shop or interaction, say, "Merci beaucoup. Bonne journée, au revoir!" (Bonne Soirée if evening). You will earn a pleased and respectful response almost every time. Learn "Desolé" [sorry] and "Pardon" (or Pardonez-moi) and use them liberally whenever appropriate. The same goes for "s'il vous plâit" and "merci." Know "de rien" and "Je vous en pris" for you're welcome. If you have had a wonderful conversation or feel especially well taken care of use, "C'était un plaisir" and for really outstanding experiences use, "C'était un grand plaisir" [It was a pleasure AND it was a great pleasure]. I never failed to get a beaming response after making either comment. Having a good handle on just these few phrases makes a world of difference.

F. Language Hacks

<u>Always start in French</u>

As mentioned, the French don't care if your language skills are poor, they just want you to try. Think about how you would respond if you met a tourist in America who immediately started talking in Chinese and then expected you to respond in kind. So, absolutely, start every conversation in French! For me, I find it useful to anticipate the conversation and think through the first couple sentences, maybe even sneaking a peek at Google Translate for assistance. Then launch in with politeness, "Bonjour, monsieur..." and try out the first couple sentences.

Apologize and Ask for Help

Unless you are fluent, you will quickly get stuck or run out of vocabulary. Smile, make light of yourself and apologize with, "Desolé je parle (or nous parlons) un peu de français." [Sorry I (or we) only speak a little French]. You can add in for good measure, "Mais j'aime essayer" [But I like to try]. If delivered in the proper tone, they will then be very patient in helping you with your French and will even correct your pronunciation. Look interested and repeat the pronunciation until you get it right. They are uniformly pleased by your efforts. If you are doing well but get stuck on a single word, ask "Comment on dit 'strawberry' en français?" [How does one say strawberry in French?] They will teach you and your French improves one conversation at a time.

Compliment when the Conversation turns to English

Once you have proven that you are doing your very best to speak the language, you have broken the ice. They will often change over to English which may or may not be very good. No matter how good or bad it is, compliment them. Use "Vôtre anglais est très bien" [Your English is very good], or "Vôtre anglais est mieux que ma français!" [Your English is better than my French!] and laugh. You often get into a good natured, comical argument, both insisting the other is better at foreign language. One thing we noticed when it comes to language is that having a good command of English is a point of pride for the French. Sometimes the sternness you feel comes from a self-consciousness on their part about not knowing enough English. If you make a joke of your own skills, it often puts them at ease.

G. Understanding the French Reserve.

I won't say much on this as I am no expert. There are many books written on the topic. But the French keep their professional and private worlds separate. They typically do not self-reveal the way Americans do with complete strangers. We tend to do this with the French, expecting them to be oh-so-interested in our personal lives. This feels uncomfortable to them (and their reaction is sometimes misunderstood as rudeness). Don't get me wrong, if you take the time to be polite and prove yourself, you will end up having delightful, personal interactions. But don't lead with the intimate details or your life story. The conversation needs to start formal and warm up first.

H. Food and Drink

This area is a minefield because there are so many unwritten rules. And to make it worse, the rules are not the same in every region or type of establishment. Food and drinks were the areas, without a doubt, where we made our biggest mistakes on our first trip.

Café Culture

Your first problem is how to get a seat. In Paris, the consensus seems to be that if you see an open table, simply sit down with confidence. There is typically no host present but a couple of busy waiters scurrying around. It will seem like they take no notice of you (but they do). Do not approach them with American anxiety (or intensity) and ask for (or

13

demand) a table. If you do, you are off on the wrong foot. There are a couple caveats to getting your table. One, if you are planning to stop only for drinks, do not sit down at a table set for a meal. Two, not all cafés play by the same rules. If you sit down and this was incorrect, they will come and tell you so. In rural France, the process seems a little different. There, making eye contact with a waiter with a casual nod or gesture toward a table is usually the right play.

When you take possession of a table, it is yours for as long as you want to drink coffee or wine. By the way, drinks are cheaper when standing at the bar. At the table, you are paying for the territory. Since the servers are paid a good wage and don't have to quickly turn over tables, it may take a while for them to come around with a menu and then a while more to come back for your order. This is not "rudeness" but just how things are done. Sit back and enjoy the view, the people watching, the scene... When you do have menus, make sure you know what you want when they return—remember they are busy. Start with "Je voudrais, s'il vous plâit..." [I would like please...]

Café as in Coffee

There are rules for coffee too, of course. When you order "un café," you are ordering an expresso in a demitasse cup. It is usually bitter and served with a sugar packet (and sometimes a little snack). If you want an American coffee, you need to ask for "un café allongé" or "un café américain." I always think when in France and order un café. The waiter recognizing me as an American will invariably ask to be sure, "Un café, un espress???" I say "Bien sûr" [of course] which usually gets a nod. Courtney prefers "un café crème" or "un café au lait." One thing to know about these two drinks is that they are only drunk at breakfast. Courtney asked for a café crème after a three-course lunch. The young waitress looked at her like she was from Mars and even had to go to the head waitress (either to see if it was allowed or to laugh at us, or both).

Money-Saving Tips

Unless you really like paying for fancy, still ("plate") or sparkling ("pétil-lant" or "gazeuse") water, don't. Plain water everywhere we have trav-elled in France tastes just fine. The fancy waters don't really get pushed on you except at more touristy spots. So, act like a Parisian and right off the bat, order "une carafe d'eau, s'il vous plâit." (You can never say please enough in France.) Because you walk so much in Paris, dehydration is an issue. So, even when stopping for a coffee or a glass of wine, always ask for a carafe of water too.

Another good tip is that house wines are almost always quite good. It would reflect badly on the proprietor if they were not. Available in red, white, or rosé by the pitcher, "pichets" come in different sizes, with prices listed on the drink menu. You will be shocked at how inexpensive pichets can be, even in Paris. If you do want to order a special wine, bottles on the menu are much cheaper than you'd pay in an American restaurant. When you don't want to split a whole bottle for lunch, then feel sluggish all afternoon, most restaurants offer some choices in 500ml bottles, perfect for about two small glasses each and more affordable.

Avoiding Tourist Traps

As mentioned, tourist trap restaurants typically surround all major attractions. Do the research to find authentic places which are often just a couple of blocks away. A dead giveaway for a tourist trap is any restaurant which prominently displays an English menu in the window. On a side note, even in authentic places, they immediately peg you as an American and hand you an English menu. They are always a little sur-prised when you politely ask if you could have the French menu instead. You can probably figure out what most things are and can use Google translate if needed. It is actually fun to order something featured you can't fully translate, try it, find it appetizing and then learn later what you ate. (As Courtney found out in Gascony!)

Ask for Recommendations

This one not only goes for restaurants but also the shopping section that follows. The French pride themselves on their knowledge of their craft. Ask your waiter or sommelier for suggestions for your choice of dish or a wine pair. There are many ways to ask this, but for me the easiest phrase to remember is, "Pourriez-vous recommender...'X'... s'il vous plâit?"

Hacks for Eating and Drinking Like an Insider

You will read blogs instructing you to keep your hands above the table at all times and to never look at your phone during a meal. Try to follow this as much as you can. However, neither is as big a deal as they are made out to be online. Maybe not quite as much as Americans, but the French love their phones too. Of note, we never took any flack for taking pictures of our food or trading bites.

One thing to be prepared for is when you order a bottle of wine, it is delivered with great ceremony, and you will be asked, "Who tastes the wine?" Decide which of you it will be. Don't try to be a wine snob—swirl it, take a quick whiff, then a sip, and pronounce it, "Très bien." It is almost always good. Another tip (and they notice when you do it right) is that your slice of the ubiquitous bread served with every course goes on the tablecloth in between bites and not on your plate. This seems odd to us, but it shows you have learned something about their culture. Another bread tip is to use the bread to sop up the rich sauces left on your plate. At the fanciest restaurant at which we ate, the waiter observed, on collecting my wiped-clean plate for one of the many courses, "I see you do it the French way."

Next, order like a local. Don't sit down and order a Coke and demand alterations to what's on the menu. This insults the chef, as does adding salt or pepper, which often aren't even on the table. Instead, order things you haven't tried before. Do a little research on typical drinks and dishes of the region. You don't have to do this at every meal, but order an apéritif before dinner and when you do, order one that is classically French. Don't order a margarita. One classic is a "Ricard" (pastis—licorice flavored liquor). I like, but don't love it, but every time I order it, eyebrows go up followed by a nod. "Kirs" are also a classic, sweet choice. In outlying regions, figure out their specialties. Later, you will read how ordering a rustic "Vin de Noix" (homemade walnut wine) in the Dordogne changed an entire experience into an unforgettable one. Be adventurous in ordering your food—it is all delicious. If ordering a steak, the proper French way is rare or even really rare. Really rare in French is "bleu." I love my steak rare and always order bleu. The waiter will check for sure, "Bleu???" Answer, "Mais bien sûr" [but of course]. If you can't do rare, they won't kick you out of the country for ordering it medium ("moyen") but you won't earn the same respect. If you order it "bien cuit" (well-done), you may well be asked to leave!

Finally, at the end of the meal after the dessert and/or cheese course, the French almost always have a coffee. After a heavy two-hour lunch, coffee makes perfect sense to me. If I have a coffee after dinner, no way am I getting any sleep! That being said, you often get a funny look when you turn down coffee. We ended up in the habit of ordering a decaf at the end of dinner (or better yet, a digestif like a Cognac or an Armagnac).

Complimenting the Meal

As mentioned, the French take great pride in their craft. You will be asked at several points how you like the meal. Always answer in the positive. The simplest thing to say for Americans is, "Très bien," but because we use it so much it can almost sound trite. Use other superlatives if you can remember: "C'était " [it was], "délicieux" [delicious], "formidable" [wonderful, tremendous], "magnifique" [magnificent] or easy ones, "excellent" and "parfait." Courtney makes fun of me for this one, but I often make sounds of delight when eating something incredible. So, I will often add an "Mmm!" while holding two fingers close to my mouth when answering with a superlative.

Paying and Tipping

This is another one which can be a maze. Waiters in both cafés and restaurants will not spontaneously bring your bill. Remember, you are paying for the territory for as long as you want it. It is easy to sit there ready to go, steaming about the "rude" waiter if you don't understand this. How to pay your bill is different at every place. The easiest is at nice restaurants where you typically ask for "L'addition s'il vous plâit?" You sometimes may signal this with a little gesture of signing your name in the air. Be careful not to let either the question or the gesture appear demanding. If it does, you might get completely ignored. If you are paying by credit card (check that they accept cards ahead of time), they will bring a portable machine to your table to complete the transaction.

At other levels of restaurants and cafés, it never seems clear how to pay. Here are a couple hacks to help. First, when you sit down, identify a table of locals around you that are a course/drink or two ahead of you and watch what they do. Here's another one I came up with. Toward the end of the meal, ask "Où sont les toilettes?" [Where is the bathroom?] Use the restroom then when walking back past the bar/register casually ask, "Est-ce que je paye ici ou à table?" [Do I pay here or at the table?] It works like a charm.

Tipping in France is something you will read about in every blog. The gist of it is this: French waiters are paid well, and the tip is already figured into the price. Sometimes the menu even states the gratuity is included. You don't have to tip at all, but it is common courtesy to leave a euro or two, the "pourboire" ("tip"—I love this word which actually translates to "for a drink" [for the waiter]). If you receive exceptional service, feel free to leave a little more. They won't refuse it, but it is not at all expected.

I. Bathrooms and Umbrellas

Two of our favorite superstitions—pack portable toilet paper and an umbrella (or pick one up on arrival) and have them with you at all times. This 100 percent ensures all bathrooms you visit will have TP and it will never rain. The one day you forget either, you are screwed. Speaking of which, every time you stop at a café, restaurant, or nice department store, take the opportunity to use the restroom, even preventively. They are typically nicer and cleaner than anywhere else. Public toilets often cost to use and are, well, not so nice. There may not be any TP in some of them. Occasionally you may even run into Courtney's nightmare, the "Turkish toilet" which is basically two plates for your feet over a port-a-potty hole. She will suffer mightily before ever using one of these again. There are even reported to be open air "pissoirs" alongside sidewalks for men in Paris, but we never saw one. I was very disappointed.

J. Shopping

Merchants

First, remember the earlier suggestions to start with a polite, formal greeting and ask for advice when you need help. French shopkeepers have very distinct opinions, which are usually spot on, especially if you are talking about fashion (you will read about the shopkeeper and a dress Courtney bought later). They may even make suggestions for accessories or other pieces to complement whatever you have picked out. Probably the biggest tip is that in most places, you are NOT to touch the merchandise. Instead, ask the keeper for assistance. If touching is okay, they will then let you know it is fine to rummage through the rack or shelves of goods. If not, they will come over and help you sort through their stock, picking out the style and size which fits you best.

Markets

Like shops, it is really important not to handle the offerings here. If you want two artichokes and half a kilo of cherries, explain what you want and then add "pour aujourd'hui," [meaning to eat today], "pour demain," [for tomorrow], or for some other date in the future. They will then give you their full attention while choosing produce of the perfect ripeness for the day you requested. They may give you suggestions about how to cook it or just strike up a conversation (even if there is a line behind you). If you are in line when one of these conversations is going on, be patient. "C'est normal."

Other market tips:

1. Get there early. The best products often sell out before noon, and you avoid the busiest times when you can literally be shoulder to shoulder all the way down the street.
2. There may be several different stands for fruits, vegetables, meat, bread, various trinkets, and clothes. Some are bigger, more commercial stands. If you look closely, they may be selling imported produce and cheap goods. Look for smaller stalls advertising family names, "straight from the farm" and artisanal products.
3. Peruse all the stands first, making note of whose stuff looks the best but also noting the ones where there are long lines of locals. This is where you should buy from. Do it before they sell out!

4. If you are not good with the metric system, work out the amounts you might ask for ahead of time—500 g is about a pound, 200-250 g about half a pound, 100 g about a quarter pound. Do some thinking about how euro/kg translates to dollars per pound and what the current exchange rate is to gauge how much you are actually spending.

Grocery Stores

Courtney and I both love foreign grocery stores which we find to be interesting windows on culture. There are a few things to know in France. Carts are usually locked up and can be unlocked with a euro coin you then get back when you return it. Produce departments vary but in many you must weigh your own produce on a scale, select the correct item on the machine and print your own label. Other places are more like America. If you aren't sure and this stresses you out, you can find some pre-packaged fruits and vegetables already with tags. All this being said, I'd still get most of your produce from a local market.

The cheese and yogurt selections are overwhelming. Often there is an actual cheese monger behind a glass case. Additionally, high quality, pre-packaged cheeses can be found in another section. Finally, there are the more industrial produced cheeses which have an entire aisle of their own (same with yogurt). Milk and eggs are most commonly not refrigerated and can be found on shelves. If you go to a supermarché or bigger yet, hypermarché, you can buy just about anything like Target or Costco. One last note on grocery stores, you will be tempted by aisle after aisle of wine from all the best regions at ridiculously low prices. If you are not a wine connoisseur, be careful. You may fill up your cart with big name wines not anywhere near old enough to be drunk that week or quite possibly "named" wines which aren't the best expression of said name which brings us to…

Wine Shops

When I think of specialty wine stores in America, I think of nicely curated collections and spending more money than I planned. In France,
you are in for a pleasant surprise, at least by our experience. Quickly
read a few reviews of nearby wine stores and pick one. Walk in with
your polite greeting and ask the merchant for suggestions. Start in
French, and apologize when you get stuck. (See a pattern here?) Tell
the merchant what you are looking for and about how much you'd like
to spend, something like, "Je voudrais deux bouteilles de vin rouge
entre quinze et vingt-cinq euros." [I would like two bottles of red wine
between fifteen and twenty-five euros.] Or if you know the appellation
you want, mention it. What typically ensues is a conversation about
what you like in a wine after which they lead you to the right section
and pick out a bottle for you. Sometimes you end up discovering a
new wine you love. The wines we bought this way were far superior to
anything I've picked out in grocery stores and surprisingly the mer-
chants often point you to very affordable choices on par with grocery
store prices.

K. The Métro, Transportation, and Staying Connected

Studying the variety of ticket options and the complicated, color-coded
map before you get there can make you cross-eyed. Worrying about
safety and proper etiquette is anxiety provoking. However, the Métro
is super easy to use, felt very safe to us, and is absolutely the best way to
get around Paris. You can Uber if you want to but expect to get stuck
in traffic and spend a lot more. This section contains some of the very
best hacks in this guide.

Navigo Easy is the "Easiest" Ticket to Use

Without getting into the complexities of various ticket options, Navigo
Easy is the way to go. You can buy the card at any manned Métro or
RER station. Just ask for "deux Navigo Easy cartes avec un carnet." You
each need one since they can't be shared on the same trip. You pay two
euros for the card and 14.90 for the carnet which is ten rides loaded to
the card. You get about a 20 percent discount over single priced tickets
which pays for the card with the first carnet. To use your Navigo Card
(it looks like a credit card), simply approach the turnstile and hold it
to the purple dot on top. As the turnstile opens, look just above the
purple dot and the number of rides left on the card shows. When you
run out, there is theoretically a way to add additional rides or carnets
with the automated machines. However, the machines didn't like our
credit cards, so we just went back to the window to have them add
another carnet.

Citymapper, Citymapper, Citymapper!

How then to navigate the maze of Métro lines? All the lines are color
coded and you need to know the name of the last terminal in the direction you are going. One use of your card allows as many transfers as
you need, including the RER lines, within the designated inner area of
Paris (which includes everywhere you'd want to go excluding airports
and Versailles). The **CITYMAPPER** app is a must. Like Google Maps,
you enter your starting and ending addresses. It will then present you
multiple options—walking, biking, Uber, buses and Métro routes. Take
a look at the suggested Métro routes and pick one out.

You may have to decide between faster routes with more transfers
or slightly slower routes with fewer transfers. It will also show you how
much walking you'll have to do to and from the stops. By the end of the
trip, we were exhausted and happy to sit on the train a little longer if it

saved us a few steps. We also tended to choose routes, if we could, which avoided the busy Les Halles station and lines that serve Gare du Nord and the northeast suburbs just for safety's sake. Both areas are known for pickpockets and petty crime.

The app is fantastic. It shows you when the next train is due and which section is the most optimal to sit in—front, middle or back. When you get to the station where you need to transfer, there may be multiple lines you can catch, each going two directions. The app makes it simple to just follow its directions with well-marked Métro signage leading the way. Knowing in which section to sit is key. If the app tells you to sit in the back, your next connection or best exit will be in the direction of the back of the train and vice versa. Most stations have multiple exits which may bring you up to town many blocks apart. The app handles all this for you. Reading this makes it sound more complex than it is. Just download CITYMAPPER and play around with it before you go. You'll get the hang of it, and it will end up saving you thousands of steps over the course of your vacation. CITYMAPPER is the bomb!

Safety on the Métro

If you have a little city sense, the Métro is really quite safe. All you need to do is be aware of your valuables and be smart. Carry your billfold in your front pocket. I have a great little trim wallet/passport holder I've used for all our trips. Ladies, take a cross body purse and keep it in front of you. If you are carrying a backpack or shopping bags, hold them in front of you as well. Don't look anxious and gawk continuously at the map of stops on the wall; it labels you a target. The crowd definitely gets a little rowdier toward midnight, but it still felt safe to us. See above for areas you might choose to avoid in an abundance of caution.

Etiquette on the Métro

This is another interesting cultural study. The first thing you will notice is how quiet it is in a crowded Métro car (the same goes for French restaurants where you barely hear a murmur). The only people talking above a whisper on the Métro are foreigners, old ladies of a certain class, and drunk teenagers. Most people don't make direct eye contact, but everyone is checking you out and sizing up everyone else on the sly. You occasionally get a very uncomfortable and unwavering stare. Pretend you don't see it and turn in another direction. There are fold down seats in the main loading areas; it is etiquette not to use these seats when the area is crowded. It is also etiquette, as it should be everywhere, to give up your seat to the elderly or infirm. When you board during busy times and are going several stops, work your way across the area to stand on the other side to stay out of the traffic.

Navigating on Foot

You could use the Citymapper app to navigate by foot, but as a long-time user of Google Maps, I find following its walking directions clearer. The important feature here is the ability to use Offline Maps. Check with your phone company for what is covered in your plan for France. Our T-Mobile plan, for example, includes free 2G coverage. For a one-time fifty dollar charge for one phone, we could get 4G coverage for 30 days which included more gigs than we'd ever use. We added this to my phone since I am the navigator. Courtney did have 2G coverage with her phone, but it wasn't great and it was SLOW! Cell coverage in Paris is excellent as you'd imagine, but downloading Offline Maps on Google still makes sense.

To do this open the app, touch your account (your initial in the upper right), and then "Offline Maps." Touch "select your own map," expand or contract the map to include the entire area you will be visiting, then download it to your phone. If your coverage fails for any reason, you can still navigate using Google Maps. This was not a huge problem in Paris but saved our butts many times in rural France when my phone would sing out "GPS est perdu."

RER and TGV trains

RER trains run on longer lines with fewer stops connecting Paris to the airports, outlying areas and Versailles. You can ride the RER lines from the airport into the city cheaply (at the time of this writing tickets were about eleven euros). We planned to ride from the airport but didn't (for reasons beyond our control as you will read in the next chapter). We did ride the RER to Versailles. There is not much to say except that it isn't difficult.

If you are travelling a distance from Paris for a week or two in another region, the TGV high-speed trains are easy to use and super comfortable. It takes about the same time, or maybe less, than airport security, waiting to board and flying. It is also cheaper. One thing we did this time was scout out the Montparnasse terminal ahead of time. We were leaving at the crack of dawn the following day and didn't want the stress of not understanding the layout. We have travelled in Europe by high-speed train twice and in both cases, first class tickets were only about twenty euros more. While I haven't been in a second-class seat, I can vouch for spacious, comfortable reclining seats with convenient computer tables and a nice view racing by the window in first class.

L. Paris Specific Hacks

We have already covered buying advanced tickets to attractions and not trying to do it all in one trip. You may have read about the Paris Pass which grants you access to more attractions than you could possibly visit for a fee that seems reasonable if you add it all up. Once we had our itinerary worked out, I calculated and for us it wasn't a good deal. I am not arguing against it per se, but add it up with your itinerary and decide if it works for you.

The Louvre's "Secret" Entrance

You definitely want to get to the Louvre before it opens and head immediately to the *Mona Lisa* if you hope to see it without an absolute crush of people snapping selfies. Early in the morning, you will see a long line begin to form at the famous outdoor Pyramid entrance. It snakes back and forth like an airport security line. Instead map to **99 Rue Rivoli** and look for the "Le Carrousel de Louvre" sign and entrance. Take two escalators down to an underground shopping mall. Walk about one hundred meters past high-end shops and at the inverted pyramid, you will find one of the lesser-known entrances to the Louvre. We arrived about twenty minutes ahead of opening and were fifth in line. Even with a little confusion picking up our audio guides, we were able to view the *Mona Lisa* relatively unmolested.

Afterward, you can leisurely tour the galleries that interest you most which, given the scale of the place, takes advanced planning. Don't miss the apartments of Napoleon III, and if you like history, the extensive antiquities exhibits housing era after era of stunning artifacts are definitely well worth the time.

What You Might Consider Skipping

You can find fabulous views of Paris from a lot of places—Sacré Coeur, the terrace of the Galeries Lafayette, the Eiffel Tower, the top of the Arc de Triomphe, and from the panoramic fifty-sixth floor viewing deck of the Montparnasse Tower. We saw the views from all these places except the Arc de Triomphe and the Eiffel Tower. Many point out the view from the Eiffel Tower is missing, well, the tower. I am sure the view from the Arc de Triomphe down the Champs-Élysées through Place de la Concorde, the Tuileries, and all the way to the Louvre is great. We chose to skip these two places because they are some of the most congested, touristy areas, and we hate standing in long lines. The tickets for the Montparnasse Tower are good anytime for ninety days after purchase. You can read about times when the crowds are low. We went in the evening after a rainy afternoon cleared up. It was still cloudy with a cool wind, but we had the deck and its great view mostly to ourselves. Maybe we missed something skipping the other two, but you can't do it all.

How to Enjoy Montmartre

No trip to Paris is complete without a visit to Montmartre, the iconic hilltop village built on a commanding hill north of Paris. Montmartre with its iconic crowning monument, Sacré Coeur, can be seen from almost anywhere in the city. Its history dates to Roman times and the martyrdom of St. Denis, the patron saint of both Paris and France. Montmartre, however, is probably best known as the Bohemian enclave of some of the most famous artists in the world during the Belle Époque. Today, Montmartre is little changed from the 19th century; the history of the place is palpable across many gorgeous sites.

To get the most out of Montmartre, you need to have a good plan. First, you have to start by either climbing the 222 stairs from the carrousel or taking the funiculaire (an inclined elevator of sorts which costs the same as a Métro ticket). Tired that morning, we chose the latter and, yes, your Navigo Easy card works. You reach the top of the stairs at the base of Sacré Coeur. This is another one of the most congested areas with people taking selfies and aggressive hawkers selling cheap souvenirs. The view is great, and Sacré Coeur is magnificent from the outside. Arriving later than planned, the mid-morning lines to go inside and climb the church tower were long and not moving. Despite being outside, the area felt claustrophobic. We took our pictures and vacated the area. Around the corner, you will find the famous Place du Tetra with its ring of touristy restaurants and starving artists offering to draw your picture. It is supposed to be rife with pickpockets but didn't feel too bad to us. The charm of Montmartre, however, is away from the congested tourist sites and instead in its quiet little lanes with lush vegetation and varied architecture. I highly recommend the walk found in the Green Guide. If we had stayed in the congested areas for more than an hour, we would have come away with a much different feel.

M. The Adventure of Driving in France

First off, in Paris, DON'T! So, if you are only going to Paris, feel free to skip this section. Driving in the rest of France feels a little wild at first, but once you understand the customs and practices, it is actually quite fun. Courtney, my passenger, may well disagree. As this was my second time driving in France, I have to say it was much easier given the (re) learning curve was not as steep. Hopefully, these observations are useful if you choose to drive in France.

Roundabouts

America only has a smattering of roundabouts. In the South, at least, no one knows how to navigate them properly. Southern politeness leads people to wave you on when it's clearly their turn and often creates long lines behind them while they endlessly wait for the entire circle to clear before entering. French roundabouts are not for the cautious or faint of heart. I learned this on our first trip. The protocol, which really works so much better than stoplights when executed correctly, is to launch yourself into the flow without any hesitation when there is the slightest of car-sized gaps. If you don't, you'll be honked at from behind.

The next issue is that many French roundabouts, especially in bigger cities, may have six or more exits veering off at vastly different angles. Google Maps is good at warning you, "At the roundabout, take the third exit." On our first trip, Courtney would watch the nav, counting the exits then declare, "Right there!" leading to an abrupt exit from the circle. The only trouble here is Google and the French sometimes have different opinions on what constitutes an exit (exits to an alley or a parking lot are sometimes not recognized by Google for example). Thus, you have to stay on your toes. In addition to having your co-pilot direct you, the other skill is to look at your nav about two or three hundred meters out. Google will show an arrow pointing vaguely in the right direction with the name of the road you want, for example arrow up and to the right to take "D403." French roads are designated "D" (départemental roads), "N" (national highways) and "A" (autoroutes/interstates). Approaching the roundabout, there is always a sign clearly showing a diagram of all its named exits. These signs help greatly. When first driving, my anxiety level was high and as I approached a roundabout, the sign would pass me by just as I thought to look up for it.

Finally, multi-lane roundabouts are a complete disaster. I know there are rules, but no one seems to agree on what those rules are. They are roughly this. You should get yourself in the innermost lane if you are travelling most of the way around, then gradually move to the outer lanes while using your turn signal to indicate you are exiting. You take the outer lane if you need the first or second exit to the right. The truth is nobody really stays in any lane or uses turn signals at all. Despite my best efforts, I still earn a honk and some cursing nearly every time.

What the Hell is the Speed Limit?

The French use remote speed cameras and have very strict alcohol limits despite serving wine at every meal (it is not unusual to see locals having what is referred to as "un petit verre" [a little glass of wine] in the morning). Thus, observing the speed limit is very important. The signage for speed limits is insane and not imminently clear to outsiders. Autoroutes are the easiest—130 km/hr (80 mph). If the limit changes due to a congested area, it is usually well marked. If it is raining, it drops to 110 km/hr. Divided highways, some of the "N" roads, are typically 110 km/hr (70 mph). Where is gets tricky is on the smaller roads. In open country, the limit is assumed to be 80 km/hr (50 mph) even if it is not marked in any way. For no apparent reason, sometimes in the country it drops to 70 km/hr. (Because there is a barn alongside the road I guess?) To make it worse, not all departments (French states) have the same speed limits. Plus, you can't trust either Google or your car's digital display of the speed limit which are often wrong. When you enter a town's city limits, the town name is displayed in black on a sign outlined in red. This means the speed limit automatically drops to 50 km/hr though there is no actual sign to indicate this. Within the city, often for long stretches, it may drop to 30 km/hr. These zones are well marked, but crawling along at 18.6 mph is painful. In almost every town, there is a flashing speed indicator warning you if you are above the limit. The silliest thing about speed limits in France occurs when you leave town. There is a sign again with the town name in black outlined in red, but now with a slash through it. The limit is now 80 km/hr but no sign actually says so. Make sense? Good luck trying to follow the law!

Additional Navigation Info

Using Google Maps almost always got us to the right place, except when I accidentally mapped us to the wrong parking lot adding twenty minutes to one of our drives (more on this later). In my gut, I knew something was off. The giveaway was something that does make sense in France. At every crossroads, there are town names and arrows pointing you in the right direction. When Google kept directing me away from the signs which said Rocamadour, I somehow convinced myself Google knew a shortcut! The town names and arrows are everywhere. They don't point you to towns fifty miles away but do show them within about twenty miles of the crossroads. So, if you ever lose your GPS mapping, as long as you have a basic sense of the geography, just follow the arrows to your destination. For example, knowing Souillac was on the route to Rocamadour, I could have followed the arrows first to Souillac then those for Rocamadour itself.

Lanes in Rural France

Roads in rural France are often serpentine and, depending on the area, bend around rivers and climb hills and mountains. They are fun to drive especially if you have a car with a little pep. One slight problem, though, is most rural two-lane roads are only about a lane and a half wide. Furthermore, the French seem to drive straight down the middle. This means that when you take a steep left curve at high speeds, you have to pray there isn't someone blindly barreling down the other side of the curve. In many places, the only way for two cars to pass is to drop a tire onto the non-existent shoulder. This isn't a problem when the "shoulder" is a meadow. It is, however, when the "shoulder" is a steep cliff with no guardrails. I am not certain, but the French lack of guardrails may be a form of population control. Worse yet are the two-way roads and bridges where clearly only one car can pass. The French have a sign for this. It has two arrows pointing opposite directions. If your arrow is bigger, you technically have the right of way. Also on one lane roads, watch out for medieval walls which jump out in front of you (more later). Lastly is the "Priorité á Droite" rule. This rule gives cars pulling onto the road from tiny, sometimes unpaved roads to the right the priority over your car speeding down the highway at eighty km/hr. We figured out late in the trip that not all routes entering from the right have this priority. You can tell the rule is not in effect if the side road has a stop sign angled such that it can be seen by both the stopped driver and yourself as you cruise on down the road.

Gas Stations

Diesel and unleaded are close to the same price in France. For reference, diesel cost $7.50-8 per gallon on this trip, and unleaded about the same. When you rent a car, you want to get the smallest one that will fit your passengers and luggage given parking is always tight. If you can rent a diesel, do so for better gas mileage. This time with Europcar, reserving a diesel cost more than the calculated savings, so I reserved a regular car. When I got there, they offered me a diesel for the same price. Bonus! FYI, diesel is also known as "Gazole" and uses yellow pump handles.

If you want to save money on gas, it is cheapest at large supermarkets. You don't have to have a membership card. Especially in rural France, finding a gas station can be iffy. Thus, I always filled up when down to half a tank at our local supermarché, Carrefour. My credit card always worked there. I am not sure why (it also happened to us in Italy), but some gas stations, typically unmanned, do not like American credit cards. So, at least based on our experience, don't try to use the pumps at Géant or Casino supermarkets and stick with Carrefour if you have one.

A LONG AND PAINFUL DAY "ONE"

nd so, our journey begins. With our melatonin sleep-shifting schedule complete with a 6pm bedtime, morning came early. I am not sure why, but our son Chad who hadn't responded to a text earlier, called back and woke me up at 12:30am. I got up to answer, startled and confused. I was able to go back to bed for another hour's sleep before the alarm sounded at 1:30am (7:30 Paris time). Courtney was already up with "day before Disneyworld" excitement for the trip. The ten-and-a-half hour morning seemed endless as we spent our time working on language skills and finishing up last minute packing. We grabbed lunch with our son Ty at a nearby restaurant and returned home to take one last shower before a long day of travel.

Ty dropped us off at the airport around 3:30pm with plenty of time to check in. We got into the international departures line which didn't look too long. However, fifteen minutes later, it still hadn't moved as the two agents struggled with foreign travelers who didn't have the proper

COVID clearance for their destinations. Our anxiety built until we realized the self-check bag line on the opposite side could also be utilized for international departures. We had no problems until we got to Atlanta.

I limped through the Atlanta airport to the international terminal on my bad hip. There, the gate was a mob scene. Not wanting to risk COVID preventing us entry into France, we were among the few in the crowd wearing masks. The flight was overbooked, and the gate clerk repeatedly begged, with increasing bribes, for people to give up their seats. When we finally boarded, there were people sitting in ours. It was an Eastern European family with small children. The father pleaded with us to trade seats so they could stay together. Courtney took one for the team and sat down in the seat near the screaming children, while I agreed to sit in the man's place many rows forward. We both took our sleep medication before we took off, but neither of us slept much on the red eye to Charles de Gaulle.

Bleary eyed, we breezed through customs and retrieved our bags in a reasonable time. Despite minimal sleep, everything was going smoothly. Now all we had to do was follow the signs to the RER train which would deposit us a couple hundred meters from our VRBO. We found the escalators to the train without issue, but everyone was literally running in the other direction. A passing woman frantically explained that the platform was being evacuated. We never found out why, but it looked serious. We made a quick exit from the area and at the next building jumped into a taxi.

The taxi driver was friendly but couldn't understand my pronunciation of our destination. I had to type it on my phone for him. He grinned and corrected me, 18 Rue Suger was "su-jere" not "su-jhay." On our trip in, we caught glimpses of the Stade de France (the site of an international soccer incident the day we left Paris), Sacré Coeur, and later the Eiffel Tower and the Arc de Triomphe as we approached St. Germain de Prés. It was surreal. Our trip which was never going to happen was right before our eyes. The taxi driver pulled down the narrow one-way street to number eighteen. We lugged our suitcases up onto the curb and started to enter 18 Rue Suger when we realized it was a dentist's office. The clerk at the desk sighed and directed us to the "other" 18 Rue Suger next door.

Our host was there to greet us and led us up two tall flights of circular internal stairs to our front door. The rental was spacious for Paris with a sitting room, a bedroom of sorts, a nice enough bathroom, and a small kitchen. It was in between two bustling areas, Place St. Michel and Rue de Buci, but on a quiet side street. Without air conditioning, she gave instructions we heard repeated at every place we stayed on the trip. Open the shutters in the morning, close them in the late morning to "trap" the cool air, and then open them again at night for a comfortable breeze. We freshened up and did a little unpacking before heading out to get the lay of the land.

The plan was to find the closest metro stop, buy Navigo Easy cards, locate the ATM nearby then walk the St Germain neighborhood. The St Michel métro stop was only one hundred meters with the ATM just across the street. Unfortunately, there wasn't a manned ticket booth, so we couldn't buy metro cards. We turned around empty handed. Being folded up in an airplane all night had not helped my hip pain nor did the uneven cobblestones. Each step was stabbing. Likewise, Courtney's feet were swollen with "kankles" and her shoes were too tight, blisters already starting. We were quite a pair. We finally made it to Paris, but we weren't sure we'd be able to enjoy it. Frustrated and tired, we decided to go back to our place and put our feet up for a while.

After a rest, we attempted the St Germain des Prés walk. We only made it a few blocks to Rue de Buci before having to abandon our plan on account of my hip. We settled for a stop at the grocery store to pick up a light dinner, and the liquor store next door for a small bottle of my first "white" Armagnac. On the way back, we also stopped at a Picard (an interesting all-frozen, ready-to-eat store adored by Parisians) and picked up a few interesting dishes. We dropped off the groceries and found a ticket booth at the Odéon métro stop, 250 meters in the opposite direction. At least we had accomplished one goal. Exhaustion and pain had fully kicked in, so we gave up the day, returned home and made a beautiful charcuterie plate. Washing it down with a cold rosé and finishing off with a snifter of Armagnac numbed the pain a little. With shutters open, Armagnac in hand, and a cooling breeze carrying the soft sounds of the city, I started to relax with hopes a good night's sleep would refresh and heal us. Drifting off to sleep, Courtney mused out loud that our time in Paris would only be complete if we met our favorite actors, Thierry Goddard and Audrey Fleurot...

3

"WE'RE REALLY HERE..."

We definitely slept well but woke to a cloudy, rainy, headache-producing morning. Courtney was up early, but I was slow to clear my head. I skipped the traditional trip to the boulangerie for fresh bread and instead gulped down coffee hoping to caffeinate my brain out of its fog. We had timed tickets to the Louvre for its opening. It was just across the Seine from us, and it wouldn't have been a bad walk if not for the steady rain. Armed with jackets and umbrellas, we made the trip without too much trouble. We skipped the long line outside the famous pyramid and headed for the lesser-known underground, "Le Carrousel de Louvre," entrance as previously described. Showing up fifth in line about twenty minutes before opening was, without a doubt, a good move. At opening, we headed to pick up the Nintendo audio guides we had reserved.

Audio guides in hand, we knew it was key to hurry to the *Mona Lisa*, so we did. The most famous painting in the world is smaller than you'd imagine. You view it at a distance with guards posted around it. The line was minimal, and we got to spend as much time as we wanted viewing it. We were glad we got there early. Later in the morning, we walked back by the gallery, and it was absolute chaos. However, it was even more chaotic the day after we left Paris. That day, a man who had disguised himself as an elderly lady in a wheelchair, complete with wig and makeup, gained access to the spot in front of the painting reserved for the handicapped. In what was to be a bizarre "climate protest," he stood up and smeared a cream cake he'd stashed in his belongings on the glass protecting the painting. As the security guards came at him, he threw rose petals at their feet while shouting that we were destroying the Earth. I can't think of a more French way to protest. And no, I am not making this up, check YouTube for the video!

It is hard to overstate the grand scale of the Louvre—652,300 square feet to be exact. Built in 1190 as a fortress at the edge of then medieval Paris, it was reconstructed to serve as the royal palace in the sixteenth century. In 1682, Louis XIV moved the royal residence to Versailles. It was Napoleon who was the driving force behind the museum modestly renaming it the "Napoleon Museum" in 1802. It was to house an impressive collection of art including the spoils of war pilfered from the rest of Europe. Most were eventually returned though many artifacts from Napoleon's conquest of Egypt remain. The Louvre continued to expand in the nineteenth century during the Second Empire.

The morning had been a bit of a blur to that point, and it was hard for me to get my bearings. I had a game plan for a few highlight galleries to hit. Unfortunately, with many galleries and passageways to other wings closed, I felt stymied. The Apollo gallery was not yet open when we passed. This was a disappointment given it was "not to be missed." One could see why peering through the closed iron gates. Fortunately, further up the hallway, the passageway to the Richelieu wing was closed, and we were forced to backtrack. When we did, the Apollo room had opened. It was definitely one of our favorites and "not to be missed." The crown jewels were on display along with dazzlingly adorned ceilings and walls painted in tribute to the history of France. It was a room which absolutely took our breath away.

We did finally make our way to the Richelieu wing and found ourselves completely alone in a gallery of Rembrandts. The juxtaposition of the mob at the *Mona Lisa* and this empty gallery of masterpieces was striking. We meandered through gallery after gallery of classic artists and then headed to the gaudy "apartments" of Napoleon III. You shouldn't miss them. But, in the end, they are a study in excess and leave you shaking your head at the ridiculous display of wealth. From there, we planned to cruise through the antiquities exhibits to see the famous Michelangelo sculpture, the *Dying Slave*, before leaving. What we didn't expect was to be stunned by gallery after gallery of artifacts from ancient civilizations—Mesopotamia, Phoenicia, Syria, the Levant and, of course, the immense Egyptian gallery. It included the largest sphinx outside of Egypt, a wrapped mummy, and the sarcophagus of Ramses III. We both agreed we could spend a whole day just in the antiquities area.

Tired, sore, and hot, we called our first audible of the trip. We had planned a long walk through the Tuileries up the Champs-Élysées to wait in line for the Arc de Triomphe and then, time permitting, maybe go shopping in the famous department stores in the Opéra district. The Louvre took longer than we planned and as the morning worn on, many of the galleries were crowded beyond belief. We decided to skip the long walk and the crowds at the Arc and headed directly to the Opéra district. On our way, we stopped in the famous courtyard of black and white pillars, the Colonnes de Buren, and the Palais-Royal Garden to snap some pictures. It was getting past noon, and we were both hungry. Walking away from our planned route, we had to change lunch plans. Here, research and the Bublup app worked their magic. There were a couple targeted restaurants in the Opéra district on our way, so we headed for the ninth by way of the second arrondissement.

Walking in Paris is the only way to truly experience the city. The scene and overall feeling change every few blocks. Frequently, you catch a glimpse of an exceptional, unexpected view. On our route, we left the glamourous first arrondissement and passed through a straight forward business district with Parisians going about their daily routine before finding our restaurant. Midi 12 was about a block from the famous department store, Galeries Lafayette Paris Haussmann. We sat on the terrace and attempted our first restaurant experience fully in French. Our French was still pretty rusty, but the servers were patient and kind. We ordered a pichet of rosé and rested our legs. The galettes were excellent— for me, smoked salmon with roe and soft cheese and for Courtney, duck confit with a carrot mousse, Cantal cheese, and caramelized onions. I finished with an almond cookie crêpe with crème diplomate vanille and fresh strawberries. With our string of lovely interactions with the people maintained, we began to question the stereotypes about Parisians.

From there Courtney went on pilgrimage to the shopping landmark, Galeries Lafayette. This 750,000 square foot department store has eight floors topped with a splendid Neo-Byzantine style dome. Courtney was in heaven! We shopped (well, I just sat anywhere I could to rest my hip) up and down the store. Despite a chilly wind, we went out on the free terrace for great views of the Paris skyline. In the end, we didn't buy much. I thought I might find a swimsuit at a discount from my favorite French designer. However, I choked on the clerk's answer that they cost 230 euros. I quickly recovered to shake my head and joke in French that the style was probably too wild for an old man. Courtney was hesitant to buy too much on our first full day. So amazingly, we made it out only buying a Diptyque candle from a bubbly sales girl and some socks for Courtney. We went across the street to the store's gourmet and home goods outpost with Courtney on a mission to find cool French salt and pepper shakers. Nothing spoke to her, so we headed out.

We walked around to the front of the Palais Garnier to take pictures of the striking opera house built at the command of Emperor Napoleon III in the 1860s. Tours were not available that day. We dropped down into the Opéra métro station to ride the Métro for the first time. There is not much to stay that I haven't already, other than the Métro is so easy.

We came to surface at the Pont Neuf stop and walked across Île de la Cité to Place Saint-Michel. There we found a pop-up market a block from our VRBO. Back at our place, we took a quick shower before heading out for dinner and drinks.

The restaurant was about a fifteen-minute walk and just to the east of Luxembourg Gardens. I wanted to leave plenty early to first find the place and then take part in the French custom of having an apéro in the early evening before late dinner reservations. The Gardens close at dusk, but we did have a little time for a brief visit to what would become one of our favorite places in Paris. We found the location of the restaurant with no problem then looked for a streetside café for a drink. Just across the street, I saw a bustling, authentic looking café, Café Madame, and steered Courtney in the direction of the one open table on the edge.

Approaching the open table to confidently claim our territory, I started elbowing Courtney in the ribs and not so subtly nodding my head in the direction of our table. She was confused, but then I whispered, "Look over there, it is Thierry freaking Goddard!" I am NOT making this up and have a picture to prove it, but yes, M. Goddard sat back-to-back with me at a café. Courtney had called her shot the night before with her joke that our trip would not be complete until we met Thierry Goddard. We tried not to gawk and decided not to interrupt what turned out to be him and his wife. I did, however, take my camera out toward the street to take a wide shot of "the café." You know, we were tourists after all! The waiter was cheerful and even took our picture. I used one of my café hacks to watch our French movie star strut inside to pay and when we were ready to head to dinner, I followed suit.

La Maison du Jardin was our first sit-down, reservation experience in Paris. The servers were professional and formal but with blunted affects—nothing to complain about but also nothing to rave about. They handed us English menus before speaking to us. Interestingly, the crowd was mostly American. (Maybe because of a high Trip Advisor rating?) This was obvious given the loud American conversations audible throughout the restaurant. The food seemed outstanding in the moment though later in the trip we realized it probably wouldn't make our top ten. Our menu for the night included starters of salmon salad with pickles and a celery mousse for me and a grilled mackerel tart with tomato marmalade for Court. Our mains were, respectively, beef with chard gratin and candied shallots and lamb pastilla with lemon, served over grilled eggplant. We did have a remarkable bottle of St. Émillion wine. Courtney had hazelnut crème brûlée with hazelnut ice cream for dessert. I was disappointed with my plate of "selected cheeses" paired with the chef's own organic jam. I wished I would have ordered a true dessert.

Walking at night in Paris is a special experience. The city of lights creates interesting shadows— the history and romance of the place are palpable. We didn't want the night to end, so we wandered our neighborhood, Rue de Buci to Rue Mazarine, and then past the spectacularly illuminated Institut de France. We crossed the Seine on the pedestrian bridge, Pont des Arts. We headed down the stairs to sit on the banks of the river in view of the Eiffel Tower, its majestic spotlight gracefully rotating. We had packed a lot into the first day and a half, but sitting there together soaking up the scene, it finally felt like the trip that would never happen was real.

SUNSET ON THE SEINE

Wiped out by 29,500 steps the day before, we slept late the next day. I grabbed a baguette and pain au chocolat from Boulangerie Liberté which we devoured with butter from Brittany and copious amounts of coffee. Our first objective after breakfast was to experience the Marais. Le Marais straddling the third and fourth arrondissements was spared Haussmann's nineteenth century rebuilding of Paris with the Grand Boulevards. As such, it has retained its old-world charm with narrow, maze-like cobblestone alleys and hidden courtyards. It is billed as a hip and happening district filled with interesting bars and cafés. Many feel it is the quintessential Parisian experience, and blogs galore sing its virtues.

We started by making the short walk to cross to the Right Bank via Pont Saint-Michel, traversing Île de la Cité. Paris has traditionally been divided into the Right Bank (Rive Droite, north of the Seine) and the Left Bank (Rive Gauche, south of the Seine). While the stereotypic differences between the two have faded some with time, they still feel very different. The Right Bank is known for power, commerce, fashion,

45

luxury and chic sophistication. It is where the Paris elite live and hang out. The Left Bank, in contrast, is intellectual, artistic, and Bohemian. It is a place for students, artists, writers and philosophers to gather and celebrate café culture. Before crossing the Seine, we stopped on one of the two islands, the Île de la Cité, for a selfie with Notre Dame in the background and pics of the Tour de l'Horlage at the corner of the Conciergerie. The Tour de l'Horlage hosted the first public clock in Paris starting in 1370. The gorgeous clock there today has been restored over time.

Our first stop was Tour Saint-Jacques, a flamboyant Gothic style, 177-foot tower. It is all that is left of the former sixteenth-century Église Saint-Jacques-de-la-Boucherie (Church of Saint James of the Butchers) which was torn down during the Revolution. It is quite a sight especially when you walk up the perpendicular Rue Nicholas Flamel. From the top of the alley is a great photo op where the tower centers on the alley's vanishing point. We worked our way down Rue de Rivoli past the enormous and ornate Hôtel de Ville (Paris' City Hall). The original wing of Hôtel de Ville was built by François I starting in 1531 and was expanded during the seventeenth century. It was burned down by the Paris Commune in 1871. The hall was rebuilt shortly thereafter and even larger. It continues to be used as the headquarters of the municipality of Paris today.

We dipped down toward the Seine for our next stop, Église Saint-Gervais, the church in the oldest parish on the Right Bank. The first church on this site was built in the sixth century. The current church was built between 1494 and 1621. Because of the length of its construction, it is of Gothic style though its façade is inspired by French classicism. The feeling in the immediate area was of absolute peace even though it is only a block each way from the busy Rue de Rivoli, Hôtel de Ville, and the Seine. We slipped through the front door into a lovely, open and airy church with brilliant stained-glass windows. There was a solemn ceremony in progress with novices singing otherworldly, monastic hymns. We stood mouths open and felt transported by this transcendent scene. I took a short video, and we are able to relive this moment in time, over and over again.

Hot, hungry, and hurting again, it was time to find a place to sit down for lunch. We navigated to one of our researched restaurants. We found it on a small street tucked behind the secluded, cobblestone square of Place Sainte-Catherine, the site of a thirteenth century priory. We grabbed one of the few remaining tables on the terrace at B.D.J. Café. Starting with our French, we once again received lovely service. We began with a pichet of ice-cold rosé, perfect for the steamy day. From the formula, Court went with a starter (smoked salmon salad) and a main (steak frites), while I went steak frites (bleu of course) and a dessert—or at least I thought so. Toward the end of the meal, the waitress asked if I wanted something that I took to mean coffee which I declined. Embarrassed later, I realized she was asking about dessert. I had to get her attention, apologize, and order my dessert—a salted caramel tart with fresh fruit and caramel sauce in an artful display. Worn out, we were happy to linger a while to catch our second wind.

We walked through the peaceful square and back to the main drag. From the Green Guide, I had read about a secret side entrance to the famous Place des Vosges through the back right corner of the courtyard of Hôtel de Sully. We walked through the gates of Hôtel de Sully, a grand mansion of Louis XIII architecture, built in 1625 by a former minister of Henri IV. The courtyard was perfectly manicured and a quiet place of solitude. We sat for a while before finding the back door hidden by vines.

Place des Vosges is felt by many to be the most beautiful square in Paris. It was opened in 1612 as "Place Royale" to celebrate the engagement of Louis XIII to Anne of Austria. It is a large square surrounded by two symmetric, arcaded pavilions: the king's and the queen's. The center of the square is filled with statues, fountains, and green space. On the warm weekend day, every inch of the grass was covered with people enjoying the sunshine. While it is indeed grand, we walked away thinking it was nice but weren't sure it lived up to the hype. Maybe it was our fatigue, the heat, or the lack of anywhere to sit, but we were underwhelmed and decided we preferred the wide-open spaces of Luxembourg Gardens.

We exited to the northeast to follow the Green Guide's route of the most famous parts of Le Marais. The sidewalks were packed, and the streets were narrow. It definitely had an old-world ambiance. There were some good photo ops, but nothing blew us away. Courtney felt the shopping, for which she had high expectations, was "meh." We did enjoy ducking into the quiet courtyard of the first library in Paris and did like the festive Rue des Rosiers. Admittedly, the scene is likely different at night, but in the end, we were disappointed in the Marais which did not feel hip or edgy that day. We left feeling certain that we were Left Bank kind of people.

Back on Rue de Rivoli, Courtney hoped a trip to the BHV would brighten her day. She was in search of the perfect straw bag and of course saltshakers. BHV is a large department store more affordable than the Galeries Lafayette and Le Bon Marché. She shopped BHV high and low and came away with nothing. It felt a little like an oversized Target. I did make my way to the men's store to find a few pairs of socks and underwear to augment my dwindling supply. I teased Courtney about my relief that after two visits to big department stores, I was only out socks (twice), a candle, and some underwear. She vowed to make up for it later.

Courtney was spent at this point, but I wanted to push on to finish our walk. The baroque Église de Saint-Paul-Saint-Louis was waiting. Situated on a spot where various chapels and churches had stood since the seventh century, the current building was started in 1627 commissioned by Cardinal Richelieu. The interior of the church was elegant. We exited out a door on the left to access the secret Passage St Paul. From there, we wandered Village St Paul and its maze of ancient, cobbled passageways with galleries and antique dealers, many of them closed. All in all, we were again a little underwhelmed. What was very cool was finding one of the last remaining remnants of the Wall of Philip Augustus—the oldest fortification of Paris built from 1190 to 1209. I would have stayed here longer to soak up the history of the moment, but this was one of the few places which didn't feel safe. We were being cased by a sinister looking character. The streets mostly empty, we exited quickly in the direction of safety.

Free of that situation, the tables were turned. I was ready to be done, but Courtney really wanted to shop for our granddaughter, Cora, at a toy store in the Marais about which she had read. No easy transit option available, it was about a twenty-minute walk. On our way, we passed the simple and somber plaque decorated with dried flowers in remembrance of the 11,000 Jewish children deported to death camps by the Nazis with the assistance of the Vichy government. Five hundred of those poor souls came from this very neighborhood. Maybe it was because of the plaque but nothing much seemed joyous to us in the toy store (and much of what was there could be found in toy stores anywhere in the world).

It was late afternoon and with our next engagement a 9pm sunset cruise on the Seine, I took a quick look at the Bublup app and convinced Courtney we should quickly try to see two more things. I thought it would be fun to take a picture of "Gigi" (Cora's name for Courtney) in front of Crêperie Gigi. An added bonus for me would be a stop on the way at "The Little Red Door," a highly rated Parisian speakeasy with uniquely crafted cocktails. When we approached the address, we first walked past it, then backtracked to a recessed red door, no sign. A bouncer was standing stiffly at the door. I "bonjoured" him and asked in French if we could go in. He looked at us skeptically and answered in a Cockney accent that he'd "have a look," instructing us to wait outside. He came back, nodded at us with a smile, and led us inside. There were quite a few seats available, so I am pretty sure he was trying to decide if the old people outside were cool enough to allow in.

The bar was the definition of "cool"—a great vibe in a dark space with old school hip-hop remixes rolling over the sound system. The bartenders were not only talented but fun and convivial. The bar's concept is appealing and so very French. They work with local farm-to-table producers to find unusual ingredients for cocktails then mix them in unexpected ways, with top shelf liquors, to produce a bizarre but divine alchemy. The menu was complete with pictures and the stories of the farm-to-table producers themselves. I chose a walnut drink which was composed of walnut shrub, whiskey, dry vermouth, and sparkling wine. Courtney had her favorite drink of the trip—a locally sourced lavender soda mixed with single cask Calvados apple brandy and vermouth. I was digging the music especially when a Paid in Full remix came on, a Kirchmann favorite. A young couple from London sat down next to us at the bar, and we struck up a conversation about the drinks. They were in town for the French Open and were surprised we weren't going. We chatted about life in London, jobs, and our son who was currently doing contract work for a London video game company. We were having so much fun we decided to have another drink, despite the hour. Court's drink was super interesting made from tomato vine eau de vie, mezcal (and vermouth). My second was beetroot mistelle with rye whiskey (and again vermouth). Cutting it close on time, we said goodbye to our English friends and thanked the bouncer for letting the old people in. We hurried to Crêperie Gigi for a picture followed by a quick Métro ride home.

With no time to spare, we were only home about twenty minutes, just enough time to freshen up and eat some cheese and a few strawberries from the fridge. We were back on our feet and 700 meters later had our seats in time for departure on our Bateau-Mouche. I had resisted the boat ride on the Seine, an ultra-touristy activity, but Courtney really wanted to do it. She was right! Our departure was timed perfectly to get great sunset shots as we navigated the river toward the Eiffel Tower. Then with night falling, we rounded the bend on the hour to see the illuminated tower start its sparkling show (it illuminates at dusk and sparkles for five minutes on the hour every hour until 1am). Despite being crammed on the boat with so many others, it was truly magical. On our way back, we were treated to views of multiple, famous riverside attractions with all their lights on—including the under-construction Notre Dame. We motored all the way around Île Saint-Louis before circling back to dock at Pont Neuf below the Henri IV statue.

Pont Neuf (the "new" bridge) is actually the oldest remaining bridge in Paris, built in 1607. It is an iconic bridge with intermittent circular nooks with seating along the sidewalk. Courtney and I grabbed one for ourselves and sat together reflecting on the day, marveling at all we had already seen. We sat there for quite a while taking in the surreal setting. We were in the heart of the city we had always dreamed of visiting with a front-row seat. Hurting again, it was a painful walk home. At our place, we treated ourselves to a Picard frozen "dinner" at 11:30pm before collapsing in bed.

5

NOT ALL WHO
WANDER ARE LOST

We were up a little earlier, and I made my trek to Patisserie Liberté. I asked for a baguette and a special pastry I couldn't quite pronounce. I used "comment on dit… en français." The cashier pronounced it and then I repeated. She said it again, and I tried once more and got a smile with a "parfait!" The pastry was indeed parfait, rolled ropes of dough with a sticky sweet sauce and nuts. Today was our day for Montmartre, and we were both excited to get there. We rode the Métro and transferred once before arriving at the Abbesses station.

Coming to ground in Montmartre, we found ourselves at the "Je T'Aime" wall where an artist has created a wall with "I Love You" written in 311 languages. We took pictures before walking toward the bottom of the hill of Sacré Coeur but got sidetracked by a macaron break. In the first chapter, I described taking the funiculaire instead of the 222 steps and our experience at Sacré Coeur, so I won't repeat it here. We didn't find Place du Tertre rife with pickpockets as is often reported, but we were also on the lookout. We weren't planning to buy art, especially with the trouble of transporting it home, but we ended up with two small palate knife oil paintings from an energetic artist who gave us his Instagram address. Following a tip we read, we exited to the southeast of the square to find a small path through Place du Calvaire which connects with Rue Poulbot. Along this route, there is a marvelous view through some perfectly placed tree branches which frame the Eiffel Tower in the distance.

Rue Poulbot dead ends near the oft photographed restaurant, Le Consulat, which was frequented by Van Gogh, Picasso, and Monet among others. Planning for a light lunch, we grabbed two take-away sandwiches from the highly rated Grenouilles sandwich shop. It started to rain lightly, so we popped open our umbrella and ate our sandwiches on the curb behind Sacré Coeur. From there, we continued our tour of famous Montmartre destinations including La Maison Rose, the Montmartre vineyards and the Lapin Agile (a cabaret visited by many famous artists and depicted in Picasso's famous 1905 painting "Au Lapin Agile").

After making a detour to find the address of our **Eatwith** host for later in the week, we returned to the quieter side of Montmartre. Following Rue Giradon to a footpath and then up some stairs, we landed at the bronze Buste de Dalida, a monument to the iconic French singer who committed suicide at the age of fifty-four. The bust is, well, busty, and the bronze is worn shiny in two strategic places. Touching the "bust" is said to bring good luck. With Courtney rolling her eyes, I channeled my inner junior high boy and participated in the tradition. Down the footpath to the right, Allée des Brouillards, we arrived at a nice little park, Square Suzanne Buisson. With not a tourist in sight, local children squealed in delight on the playground and pétanque courts stood at the ready. In between was a statue of the third-century martyr, St. Denis, holding his severed head. This may seem odd in a playground but makes perfect sense to the French. St. Denis, the former bishop of Paris, is the patron saint of France.

Exiting the park on the opposite side, we jogged left a couple blocks to find Villa Léandre, a block long, dead end neighborhood with gorgeous art deco homes. Walking through the quiet, everyday neighborhoods of Montmartre in full bloom was joyful. Colorful flowering vines grew naturally on walls and out of cracks in ancient stairways. We worked our way back to Rue Lepic and wound around to the Moulin de la Galette, a windmill which has stood for 600 years (now a restaurant). From there, trying to map to the famous restaurant Café des Deux Moulins, I got us lost for a bit. Getting lost was just fine. Because of it, we wandered into the art nouveau church, Église Saint-Jean de Montmartre, and also saw another carrousel. I think Paris must have more carrousels per capita than any other city in the world.

We love the cult classic French movie, *Amélie*, which was shot all over Paris. Café des Deux Moulins is the place where Amélie worked. Much of this quirky movie was shot on location at the café. It was a hot afternoon, and I suggested we stop in for a cool drink and some pictures. Though the terrace was full, it was not busy inside, so we took a seat at a table. We greeted the staff with appropriately amiable bonjours, and I nodded at both the man behind the bar and the waitress who breezed past our table. In both cases, we were met with silence and glares, and then completely ignored. A French couple who sat down well after we arrived was promptly served. No one had even approached us with a menu. We decided we didn't have time for people like this, took a few pictures, then got up and left. It was one of the only unpleasant interactions we had in Paris.

Leaving that experience behind, we made it down to the Moulin Rouge for the obligatory tourist pictures. We did not go in. We walked down Blvd. de Clichy bordering the "former" red-light district of Pigalle. Everywhere you read that the area is gentrifying, hip, and becoming a safe place to live. I say "former" because Blvd. de Clichy still has some gentrifying to go. Every other establishment on our walk to Rue des Martyrs was an adult store. We made it to our turn and took a right. Courtney was looking forward to this destination. Based on the book, *The Only Street in Paris: Life on the Rue des Martyrs*, by Elaine Sciolino, she was excited to experience a true Parisian Street.

Surprisingly, Rue des Martyrs was a place than didn't hit with us. To be fair, we were there on a Sunday afternoon and while many stores were open, many others were not. And turning the corner onto the road, the sky darkened, and it began to rain. The radar showed a passing shower, so we decided to duck under a covered terrace to claim a table at a cute café decorated in pink, Maison Popeille. Starting all in French and using all our polite tricks for positive interactions, it ended up being a wonderful experience. The staff was attentive and friendly. Our waitress was obviously training a young woman who spoke little English. She, in particular, was happy with our French. Courtney ordered a glass of red and a snack of grilled eggplant with pomegranate seeds drizzled with several savory glazes. Thirsty from walking all day, a beer sounded good to me. I tried, in my best French, to ask about the styles of the three beers on the menu. The young waitress struggled with my question and in the end had to go ask the bartender for descriptions. The answers were lost in translation, so I just picked one. It was my own fault I didn't like it. I already knew most beers found in France are either from Belgium or have that Belgium yeast flavor to which I have an aversion. At least it was cold and wet.

We watched another, clearly, American couple opposite on the terrace. It played out like a parody skit. They were there when we arrived. We took note of them when their loud Southern accents boomed out in demanding tones, all in English. I watched with amusement as their interaction went "south." After several ignored, waving gestures turned the man's face crimson, he got up and walked part way up the main aisle and stood with his arms crossed. He wore a ridiculous, try-hard straw hat better suiting for a beach in the Bahamas (obviously picked out by his wife). He had on an embroidered Tommy Bahama, short-sleeved shirt with a garish scene of liquor pouring into a glass with the caption, "I Make Pour Decisions." To complete the look were cargo shorts and a large 'Merica tattoo on one of his calves. They let him stand there for quite a while before slooowly allowing him to pay his bill. His wife with Southern helmet hair, too much makeup, and a sundress she probably shouldn't have been wearing sat in the corner shaking her head while shooting dirty looks at all who met her eye. Pinned in a tight corner, she barely made it out as the other customers ignored her attempts to exit.

We continued to work our way down the street. Courtney bought a comfortable but stylish pair of shoes from a pleasant saleswoman. We bought some beauty products and some cute French pacifiers for Cora from a pharmacy. While Courtney was shopping, I had a bizarre experience. A couple was walking toward me and a flash in my mind told me the woman looked familiar. "Not possible," I told myself in Paris. Then, I heard, "Dr. Kirchmann?" It was a resident I had worked with many years ago. She introduced her husband, and we chatted about their trip and discussed her practice in Durham. It was their first day in Paris. Crazy!

We had planned to shop for most of the day down the length of Rue des Martyrs, before heading over to our dinner reservation three blocks from the end of the road. However, there was so little open on the street, we quickly got to the end with three hours to kill. Too far to go all the way home, we called another audible. Les Passages Couverts de Paris (Covered Passages) are a vestige of the past and, in a way, the precursor of the shopping mall. Starting in 1799 and built mostly during the first half of the nineteenth century, the city of Paris created a series of covered shopping arcades. These pedestrian passages were typically a block or more long, connecting two streets. They were built with sublime (sometimes stained) glass ceilings with ornate, iron lattice work. They were initially lit with gas lights and lined with privately owned shops, cafés, and bistros. Done in art nouveau and neoclassical architecture, these eye-catching structures were where the rich went to shop, eat and be seen. There were, at one point, 150 passages and "galleries." Several remain in all their splendor, and a few were within walking distance. We were able to experience in succession Passage Verdeau, Passage Jouffroy, and Passage des Panorama. Again, being Sunday and now evening, most of the shops were closed, but nevertheless, the awe-inspiring architecture and the detailed ceilings and floors were a marvel to behold.

With most stores in the Passages closed, we made our way back to the restaurant hoping to find a café for an apéro. We walked into a highly rated English pub next door to the restaurant, but it was 100 percent men yelling at televisions showing a soccer match. Court suggested we go back to the bar at our restaurant, "Poni", the walls of which were open to the outside. Courtney ordered a Spritz St. Germain which was delicious. Knowing we'd have wine with our dinner, I just ordered a small beer. The waiter joked in French suggesting I was a wimp for ordering a baby beer. So, of course, I was forced to order a larger one. It was a local IPA, a rarity, and a pretty good one at that.

We were given our choice of tables in either the main first-floor dining room or a cozy back room up a few stairs. We chose the latter. It had odd wallpaper with an animal motif and did feel cozy until it filled up, after which it became warm and a little claustrophobic. We were excited for this restaurant given its top rating. The food was very good. The service was competent and attentive. For starters, Courtney had white asparagus with Comté cheese, chorizo, apples, walnut condiments, and black pepper aioli. I went with the Paté of the House which included duck and free-range pork. For a main, Courtney had octopus risotto with creams of peas and green asparagus with feta shavings in a walnut reduction. I had steak tartare with black olives and candied tomatoes. A high quality Haut Medoc paired nicely. For dessert, I had Brioche Perdue ("Lost Brioche") with caramel, Chantilly cream and vanilla ice cream. Courtney had millefeuille (often referred to as a "Napoleon" in America) with light cream, pralines, and strawberries. A long time "Napoleon" fan, Court was disappointed in this one.

We did see another "Ugly American" incident. A couple sat down two tables over and once they got their menus, they did not look happy. When the server approached, we could hear the woman whine in English, "Why can't you just make me a green salad?" The menu was apparently too adventurous for her. After the waiter shook his head indicating they did not cook to order, the couple got up and left. After two such incidents on the same day, you could see where the American stereotypes come from. We rode the Metro home. In our exhaustion, we absent-mindedly took a wrong turn on the next street over from us, Rue Serpente. It was not the last time we would be snakebit by this road. We finally limped home after another long but excellent day.

6

DOG POOP PICNIC (PART 2)

Dark clouds looming, I woke with a migraine. We were running late, so we skipped breakfast and just went with coffee (and a Red Bull for me trying to clear my head). Our first stop today was Sainte-Chapelle, the astonishing Gothic cathedral commissioned by Louis IX in 1238 to house relics from the Holy Land including the Crown of Thorns, purchased at great cost. It was a short five-minute walk from our place. We were surprised to find the intersection barricaded at Pont Saint-Michel. The place was crawling with police cars and vans. The barricades were manned by patrolling guards in full gear—flak jackets and machine guns. I was worried we couldn't get to Saint-Chapelle, which was between the barricades, but we eventually saw a gap where guards were scrutinizing passports and tickets before waving people on. The Palais de Justice de Paris is within the complex. We later learned the security was for the ongoing trial of the only surviving terrorist of the coordinated attacks on Paris in November 2015.

I really have no idea what to write about Saint-Chapelle; words simply cannot do it justice. Superlatives are too tame to capture the soaring majesty of the astounding stained-glass windows. Blues and purples dominated in the morning light while the altar and elevated ambo stood in shining relief. The fifteen stained glass panels tell the story of the Bible while, in the back, the famous Rose Window depicts the apocalypse. It is a place that simply takes one's breath away. I ended up finding a bench to sit and gather myself. Courtney joined me, and we sat in stunned silence. It ranks near the top of the best things we saw in Paris. We took a ton of pictures which tell the story better than I could ever hope to, so I'll stop at that. We didn't want to leave but eventually wandered out in a bit of sensory overload.

We had combination tickets for the Conciergerie—the castle turned courthouse then prison during the Revolution. Marie Antoinette, Robespierre, and many others spent their last days here before facing the guillotine. The self-guided electronic tour was well done. With my love of history, I think I liked this one more than Courtney. A large part of the building was available to tour though the rooms were mostly bare leaving the audio guide to explain the historical significance of each location. In the end, buying the combination ticket didn't cost much more and was well worth the extra euros. We exited on the opposite end of the barricades and planned to cross the street to tour the rest of Île de la Cité. Crossing the street inside the barricades, Courtney accidentally bumped into one of the paramilitary guards and got her backpack caught on the end of his machine gun! After her apology, he waved Courtney on with a smile. I was just happy she didn't end up back in the Conciergerie awaiting the guillotine.

From there the day went downhill. Walking through the nineteenth century Marché aux Fleurs, the Île de la Cité flower market, a misty rain kicked in. Next, we planned to walk through the "ancient quarter" with hopes of a side view of Notre Dame. With the rain picking up, we sat down at a café for some caffeine. It was cool that our table actually straddled what is left of the foundation of the Gallo/Roman wall behind which the people of Lutetia took refuge from the first barbarian invasion in 285. The rest of the ancient quarter was a bust though; the gloomy rain continued, and the side view of Notre Dame was completely covered with a construction drape. We walked around to the front of the island and then across to Île Saint-Louis, but almost all the views of Notre Dame were obstructed. I was frustrated (and hurting again) but at least ice cream at the famous Berthillon on Île Saint-Louis would cheer us up.

Monday on Île Saint-Louis was completely dead. Given the dreary day, we didn't find it as charming as it is often described. Then, halfway down the main avenue, we found Berthillon- CLOSED! Two hungry, wet wanderers, one with a migraine, was not a good recipe. The plan after ice cream was to cross the bridge and walk the Latin Quarter before having a picnic lunch in Luxemburg Gardens- maybe the rain would clear? Just as we made it into the Latin Quarter proper, it started to rain hard. Standing on a street corner without cover, I quickly scanned my phone for some of my targeted restaurants in the area. Each one near us was CLOSED! We were snappy with each other and ended up grabbing a seat at the closest open restaurant with a decent rating, an Italian pizza joint. The food wasn't bad, but we were both hangry and the idea of eating Italian pizza for one of our meals in Paris was downright depressing. We debated what to do next but couldn't agree. I wanted to press on with our tour of the Latin Quarter- rain be damned. Courtney wasn't hot on this idea but reluctantly agreed. On this rainy day, the Latin Quarter was definitely historic but gray and not very pretty. Our mood was not improving. A full day in Paris was starting to feel ruined. We thought we would duck into Église Saint-Julien-le-Pauvre for a respite from the rain but found it closed until 2pm! It was 1:45. We sat down in the nearby pretty garden under some cover and tried to talk it out. We made up, laughing that this was our "Dog Poop Picnic" day for the trip (a similar frustrating tale from our first trip to France). We backtracked to the church. It was built in Romanesque style in the thirteenth century. The interior was peaceful (and dry!).

We were near the famous bookstore, Shakespeare and Company, and Courtney wanted to stop. Like many famous sites, it has become a tourist destination. When we arrived, there was a line about fifty deep waiting to get in. We passed on waiting in line and moved on to the strikingly bizarre Église Saint-Séverin. It was the first church on the Left Bank, initially built here during the Merovingian era ~650. That church was destroyed during the Viking invasions. The current structure was started in the thirteenth century, but after a fire, was rebuilt and enlarged in the fifteenth to seventeenth centuries in flamboyant gothic style. It has unusual architectural features including carved columns in a double ambulatory which surround an unusual, central twisted pillar. Gargoyles decorate the exterior. Most of the stained glass is from the fifteenth century, but the south chapel has a series of modern art, stained-glass windows produced between 1875-1900. It all adds up to a riotous style that somehow works.

We walked past the Cluny Museum of the Middle Ages and the Sorbonne on a hopeful trip to Luxemburg Gardens. We were kidding ourselves, though. With the rain continuing, a picnic today was not in the cards. Walking back to our place, we passed the other side of the museum where you could view Roman baths through the fence. The Cluny did not make our itinerary this trip but is definitely on our list for the next one. We retreated to our place to decide what to do with the rest of this fateful afternoon. We had planned to go up in the Montparnasse Tower to the fifty-sixth floor viewing deck that evening before dinner. I made the case to go since the weather was starting to clear a little, and there weren't a lot of other slots where we could fit it in. Courtney wasn't sure it was a great idea but went along for the ride.

The Montparnasse Tower on a chilly, overcast but no longer rainy day turned out to be a great decision. I am sure the view is more impressive in brilliant sunlight or at sunset but certainly more crowded. We hopped the Métro there with no problem and found the "line" for the tower elevators. At first, we were the only people in line. Eventually, another couple joined us in the elevator. Both the indoor viewing floor and the upper outdoor deck were practically deserted. You could see Paris laid out in front of you in a panorama. As a lover of cartography, it was literally a Google map with the satellite filter on. In every direction we looked, we could pick out iconic Parisian landmarks. We traded off taking pictures with a friendly French family on the lower floor and another couple on the upper deck where cool picture props were set up. It was cold and windy, but there were covered, comfortable seats and wind screens. On our exit, we crossed the street to scout out the Montparnasse TGV terminal from which we would leave Paris a few days later.

Back home, we had a little time. Courtney decided a short nap would help. I went out on a mission to visit a cool wine shop I had read about, "La Dernière Goutte." It was owned and run by an American who curated an extensive collection of wine. I entered expecting to speak English only to find myself alone in the store with a French lady. I gathered myself, starting polite and formally, and explained I was looking for two bottles of red wine between twenty and thirty euros to drink this week. What ensued was an engaging conversation starting with what I liked in wine, where we were staying, for how long, and where we were from. Strangely her father had lived briefly in Salisbury, North Carolina, and she had visited once. She asked me about politics in America, and we both ended up shaking our heads at the current state of affairs. She was informative and decisive while picking out the wine. I thanked her and told her it was a great pleasure to talk with her. She beamed and said it was for her as well. She wished me a good trip. I walked out with two fantastic bottles, one a memorable expression of the Northern Rhone appellation, Saint-Joseph.

Having spent more time at the wine shop than planned, I woke Courtney up late. We quickly freshened up, then headed for the St-Michel RER station. Hurrying through an alley near Place Saint-Michel, I almost stopped dead in my tracks at the site of a man with a guitar on his back. It was "Luc," the character actor with crazy white hair in

"Emily in Paris." As I looked at him, he nodded with a proud grin which said, "Damn right that's who I am!" Behind me by a few steps, Courtney raced up and said, "Did you see who that was!" We laughed again at our movie star sightings. On our way home, we saw "Luc" again, this time eating pizza with friends on the terrace of a restaurant a block from our place.

We almost walked past our tiny restaurant, "Le Coup de Torchon." This was one of my first calls from America for reservations. I remember the responses coming at me in the ultra-rapid Parisian French, the kind you never quite get used to. Hanging up, I wasn't entirely sure I had successfully navigated the call. Walking in sheepishly, I said, "Nous avons une réservation pour deux?" There were only six tables, and the waiter who spoke and dressed quite formally, nodded, and led us to the lone open table. I picked the place because of reviews extolling top-notch, traditional cuisine at an unbelievable value. The restaurant did not disappoint! We started with apértifs, a Ricard for me and a Peach Kir for Courtney. We ordered off the three-course formula. We picked a nice bottle of St Émillion for dinner. For starters, Courtney had house made country terrine, and I chose salade composée with avocado and smoked salmon. For mains, Courtney went with veal paupiette with a cream sauce and mushrooms. I was excited to try boeuf bourguignon mijoté à l'ancienne ("simmered the old way"). The hearty beef chunks in the stew melted in your mouth. Desserts lived up to the first two courses—crème brûlée au rhum ambré (amber rum) for Court and a brownie with sauce au chocolat for myself. The total for the bill came to about seventy dollars. (Or about what a bottle of St Émillion would cost in an American restaurant!)

After the heavy dinner, we chose to walk the twenty minutes home. And of course, halfway there, it started to rain. Hopping from awning to awning attempting to stay dry, we ducked into a Monoprix to buy a few essentials, including some blister supplies for Courtney's ailing feet. We were home by 10:30. Sterilizing a needle in a flame, I performed surgery on a particularly nasty blister swabbed with iodine. We didn't buy anything to sterilize it with at the end. Thinking quickly, I grabbed the white Armagnac and dabbed it on the wound. Legend has it that Armagnac is a cure for forty different health maladies. We can confirm bad blisters are one of them. By morning, Courtney's foot looked much better, and she was ready to face another marathon day.

CYCLING WITH THE SUN KING

W e were to meet Blue Fox bicycle tours at a Starbucks across town near a Métro stop. We were cutting it close, but after two transfers on the subway and choosing the wrong exit, we arrived just in time to head out with the first tour grouping. Vanessa was our guide and explained the process. They took care of every detail. We were given a ticket for the RER train to the town of Versailles. During the half-hour ride, Vanessa made it around to get to know each couple. She was energetic and bubbly. Actually Italian, her husband was French, and her English was excellent. Exiting the train, we headed to the large outdoor market between the SNCF station and the castle grounds. We were given a half hour to pick up items for a picnic lunch later on the grounds of Versailles. To save time, Courtney and I split up the task and ended up with a haul. I asked the cheese monger for suggestions for cheeses for a picnic. She proceeded to hand-select four different slices for me. At another stand, I bought strawberries, cherries, and apricots again hand-selected by the merchant. I finished off my purchases with one of my favorites, black pepper sausage. Courtney was proud to have navigated her purchases all in French bringing back a baguette and a bottle of Haut Medoc. We even had time to have a coffee before heading to the bikes.

We rode onto the grounds of the castle and began our tour by biking around the left prong of the mile long, cross shaped Grand Canal. The path was level and easy pedaling. I was happy to learn that biking did not bother my hip in the least. Over the course of the afternoon, we got to know the others in our group who were largely American though there were couples from Canada and Ireland as well. At the end of the left prong, we dismounted for a rest break and a history lesson from Vanessa. During her talk, a man loitering at a distance walked up and sat down uninvited to listen. I am fairly certain he had a mental illness. She asked him to leave, but he declined in histrionic fashion. She rolled with it and continued her history talk before leading us on our bikes to the far end of the Grand Canal.

The picnic spot was perfect with long views of the castle down the canal. The spectacular fountains were running, which only happens a couple days per week. Vanessa continued our history lesson while we tore into our lunch from the market. All the exercise led to a healthy appetite, and we almost finished all we bought. After lunch, we continued to bike around the Grand Canal to the Grand Trianon, Louis XIV's "summer palace." This was a "smaller" palace where he could relax, escape his court, and entertain his mistresses. It was later remodeled by Napoleon III who spent time there but never dared to live in the main palace. It was a bit of a walk from our bikes. The members of the group were free to tour at their own pace. With me limping, we brought up the rear. Not wanting to hold up the group, we hurried through faster than we wanted to. Courtney really loved the style of the interior design.

After a short ride, the Petit Trianon and the Queen's Hamlet were our next destinations. The Petit Trianon was originally built during the reign of Louis XV for his mistress, Madame de Pompadour. She died before its completion. Thus, it was occupied for a time by her successor mistress, Madame du Barry. When Louis XVI acceded to the throne in 1774, he gave the château and the surrounding grounds to his nineteen-year-old wife, Marie Antoinette. The princess from Austria (one of France's biggest enemies at the time) never really fit in at court and was not well liked by the people of France. She found the formalities of court stifling. She escaped the pressures of being queen by isolating herself at the Petit Trianon. No one was allowed to enter the property without her express permission which alienated her even further from the court and the people of France.

In 1783, on the grounds of the Petit Trianon, she commissioned the building of the Queen's Hamlet. An entire replica of a Norman village was constructed with ten quaint town buildings and a working farm. With interests in nature, she was able to play at being a "peasant" farmer. None of the products produced were ever consumed outside the royal table. The bizarre, pretend village feels like a Beauty and the Beast re-creation in a Disney theme park. Never truly understanding the queen, the people saw the hamlet as an excessive waste of money. Meandering through the little village with smells of sweet clover wafting in the air did feel like a fairy tale, but you could see why the extravagant, "fake" village was not well received at the time.

We rode out of the palace grounds to deposit our bikes and say goodbye to Vanessa who then handed us our tickets to the main castle to tour at our own pace. Versailles is a place, like Saint-Chapelle, which is hard to describe in all its splendor. I think most have seen pictures of Versailles, but nothing prepares you for the immensity of the place. We walked through room after room, lavishly decorated wall-to-ceiling with dramatic works of art. Many of the rooms were named after planets (because, of course, everything revolved around the "Sun King"). The king's bedroom was near the center of the castle where hundreds would gather to watch and assist him as he rose from his sleep to dress. Part way through the tour, the crowd felt stifling, and in the heat, Courtney felt faint. We escaped to a corner with an open window to regroup. After a few minutes in the cool breeze, Courtney rallied, and we were ready to move on to the star attraction.

All of the lavish rooms at Versailles pale in comparison to the Hall of Mirrors which is a truly amazing site. Measuring 240 x 34 feet and 40 feet tall, it boasts thirty audacious paintings in the vaulted ceilings celebrating the power and glory of Louis XIV. It derives its name from the seventeen enormous floor-to-ceiling mirrors (made of 357 individually mirrored surfaces) on the interior wall of the great hall. Opposite are seventeen arched windows looking onto the garden, the iconic Apollo Fountain, and down the length of the grand canal. Suspended from the ceiling are forty-three enormous and elegant chandeliers. At a time when having even a single, high-quality mirror was a sign of great wealth, the hall was built to project the power, authority, and superiority of Lous XIV and France. Later, it served as the backdrop for numerous historic events. The treaty to end the American Revolutionary War was signed here. After France's humiliation in the Franco-Prussian War in 1871, German bands paraded on the grounds of Versailles while Kaiser Wilhelm was proclaimed the emperor of a unified Germany in the Hall of Mirrors. And in a case of turn-about is fair play, the Treaty of Versailles ending World War I was signed here, imposing harsh penalties on a German state that would rise again. Standing at one end taking in the grandeur and contemplating the history of the place, it was a special moment for both of us.

Our trip back to Paris was comfortable and smooth. We stopped along Rue de Buci for an apéro before retiring home. After a big lunch and a full day of exercise, we were content to finish off the leftovers from our picnic. It was still pretty early, and we were tempted to go out on the town. But fatigue overrode this idea, and we called it a night—after another full day.

8

MIDNIGHT IN PARIS

Wednesday, we had strict instructions to meet Alex, our photographer, at eight o'clock sharp. We were to meet at the Trocadéro, the Right Bank park which looks across the Seine to the Eiffel Tower. The photo shoot was a Christmas present from our daughter and son-in-law, Kelsey and David—an extra thank you for caring for Cora throughout the pandemic. Alex met us promptly at the appointed time. He asked if we wanted to speak French or English. Our language skills improving, we went with mostly French though flipped back and forth when needed. We discussed our lives and his—he was born in Corsica but lives on the outskirts of Paris. He schedules three to four shoots per day. Taking his clients to six or seven different locations each, he logs 26,000 steps a day. It was fun to be on a photo shoot at the Eiffel Tower, though as Courtney will attest, my skills at posing for pictures are God awful (though slightly better than my dance moves). Unfortunately, after going at it hard all week, the close ups showed two tired travelers (including one aging, gray-haired man). I am glad he took like a thousand pictures because a few actually turned out nicely.

Next up for us were timed tickets to the Musée d'Orsay, the grand, Left Bank art museum in a former Beaux-Arts railway station built at the end of the nineteenth century. The d'Orsay houses the largest collection of Impressionist and Post-Impressionist masterpieces in the world. Many will tell you that if you had to pick from either the Louvre or the d'Orsay, you should pick the latter. With extra time built into the itinerary, we rode the Métro to near the museum, then found a café for some baked goods and much needed coffee.

The Musée d'Orsay is another French landmark where a laundry list description just doesn't cut it. We started on the top floor at the giant, see-through clock which was featured in the 2011 movie *Hugo*. We were able to get a couple shots of Courtney all alone with the clock before the crowds descended upon us. We are both drawn to Impressionism, but neither of us knows a ton about art. Of note, the audio guide here is very informative (and inexpensive). For us, the extensive Monet collection stood out, of course, as did that of Pissarro. One surprise for Courtney was how taken she was by the works of Alfred Sisley. There were two full rooms featuring Van Gogh and for me, it was interesting to follow the ups and downs of his mental illness simply by the composition of each piece.

Working our way downward and the clock approaching noon, the crowds grew in intensity. There were incredible exhibits on every floor not to mention that the Beaux-Arts train station is itself a spectacular work of art. However, at some point, we hit sensory overload combined with a bit of claustrophobia. My hip was at it again, and I was struggling from too much time on my feet. It was time to leave, but we both agreed this was a place where we'd like to return when crowds are low and spend more time.

Next, we planned to shop the nearby, famous market street, Rue Cler, but first hunger called. Scanning the research on our app, we headed for Le Florimond, a restaurant at the top of my list near Rue Cler. It was certainly walkable, but this was a time when a quick Métro trip saved us a few hundred steps, so we chose to ride. In retrospect, Le

Florimond was one of our top five (or maybe top two) meals on the trip. We have since vowed to return on every subsequent visit to Paris. Not only was the food superb, the staff, from top to bottom, was one of the friendliest we encountered anywhere. We secured a table on the small terrace and settled in for a lunchtime gourmet extravaganza.

The meal began with a starter plate trio, artfully arranged. Mixed paté sat next to an attractively prepared salad. The salad contained melt-in-your-mouth flakes of mild white fish, beans, and our first exposure to sea asparagus, our new favorite ingredient. This dainty plant really does taste like salty asparagus. It grows both in marshes and amongst seaweed. At the far end of the plate were yellow peppers, carrot shreds, and a cherry tomato, pressed into a mold and swirled with a flare. Courtney was going with seafood for her main, so we ordered a small bottle of one our favorite whites, a Sancerre. This paired well with her delicate cod fillet served with smoked eggplant in an elderberry butter sauce. I went with fall-off-the-bone tender, braised pork ribs with peapods and potatoes in a delicious, unusual barbeque sauce which can only be described as French. For dessert, Court chose pineapple compote and mango sorbet with passion fruit sauce. I had one of my favorite desserts of the trip, a dark chocolate quenelle covered in apricots and muscovado crumble. Afterward, we sat and savored the experience with coffee that came with little post-dessert snacks—lightly flavored meringues and little chocolate biscuits.

After lunch we did make it to Rue Cler. As with most markets which start to close down by late morning, afternoon wasn't the best time to visit. Rue Cler is super cute but dominated by vendors of many different specialty food products. Just coming from a heavy lunch and staying across town made food purchases impractical. But there were some nice shops too. Courtney enjoyed picking out a stylish Armor-Lux scarf at one of the shops. Just down the street, with the assistance of an opinionated shopkeeper, she bought Cora a dress and hat at Le Petit Bateau.

Having skipped much of our own neighborhood the first day, we rode the Métro a few stops to Église Saint-Sulpice in Saint-Germain-des

Prés. It is near Luxemburg Gardens and a short walk from our place. The church is easily recognizable by its two impressive towers which are mismatched and asymmetric. Built in the 1600s on a twelfth century foundation, it is one of the largest churches in Paris. It features mural paintings by Eugene Delacroix. With a soaring vaulted ceiling, dazzling stained glass, and what is considered one of the world's most magnificent organs, it has a lot to offer. We were struck by a side chapel dedicated to the victims of COVID-19 with hundreds of poignant pictures of loved ones lost to the pandemic. On the tribute wall was a quote to remember, "Un monde sans mémoire est un monde en danger." (A world without memory is a world in danger.)

Many of you know this church from the book and movie, *The Da Vinci Code*. In 1728, an English clockmaker was hired to build a special type of sundial right into the church. Courtney spotted the inlaid brass line running across the church floor. At exactly noon, a hole in one of the southern stained-glass windows casts a beam of light onto the brass line. As the season changes, the beam travels back and forth on the bronze line shining on a tall obelisk at the winter solstice and ending at a plaque in the floor opposite at the summer solstice. *Da Vinci Code* author, Dan Brown, worked this into his tale of the Templars giving it the fictitious name, The Rose Line.

From there we walked to Luxembourg Gardens. The gardens and palace were built in the early 1600s at the request of Marie de Medici, the widow of Henri IV and at the time the regent for her son, King Louis XIII. She built Luxembourg Palace, her new residence, to resemble Pitti Palace in her native Florence. The palace now serves as the site for the French senate. The gardens are artistically landscaped with large open spaces, tree-lined paths, tennis courts, and the famous Grand Basin with its model sailboats catching the wind. A nice day, the multitude of chairs were filled with Parisians relaxing and enjoying the sun. Children with long, thin sticks scrambled to redirect the sailboats crisscrossing the basin. Though we had explored a small corner of the park near closing time earlier in the week, this was our first view of the Grand Basin with the palace as its backdrop. Looking for the best angle for pictures, I sat down on a bench (apparently too close to a group of elderly locals). I didn't notice, but Courtney was sure they were annoyed. Annoyed or not, one of them chased us down after we exited to return our camera which I left sitting on the bench!

Our last activity of the day was dinner in the home of a Parisian local. **Eatwith** is a website which is basically the Uber or Airbnb of home-cooked meals. You enter your dates, read reviews, and look at pictures of the food before requesting to eat with a local. Claudine, who lived in an apartment in Montmartre, was our choice. Before heading to Montmartre, Courtney wanted to freshen up at home. We had decided on flowers as an appropriate gift to offer our host. With Courtney getting ready, I walked across the bridge to the flower market on Île de la Cité. I had to detour around the barricades to get there. On our first visit to the market, I hadn't noticed that most of the flowers there were potted and not cut flowers. I walked up and down the stalls looking for an appropriate gift. At a shop with a few cut flowers, the flower lady was busy chatting with a friend. I thought it would be smart to ask which bouquet would be most appropriate for a French dinner party. She didn't give me much of an answer and waved me off with a gesture toward the section where I was already standing. I grabbed a bouquet which turned out to be chrysanthemums and also bought three unusual, painted orange roses for Courtney.

Before leaving, I, thankfully, read online that mums are strongly associated with death in France. It is considered a faux pas to offer them on any occasion other than a funeral! Though not a large bouquet, we took Claudine the orange roses I bought for Courtney. Arriving a few fashionable minutes late, we met Claudine who greeted us warmly and thanked us profusely for our small bouquet. As most apartments go in Paris, her place was small. It was cute and well set up to use the space efficiently. Claudine was an awesome host. A former English teacher in

France, she had traveled several times to the United States and loved America. We were excited to practice our French, and she was pleased with our efforts. We were a little disappointed to hear she was expecting one other couple for the dinner party, also American. Claudine spent the rest of the night speaking English given the other couple spoke little French. That couple was from Michigan though had lived in Wake Forest, North Carolina for a time. She was a retired college librarian, and he had worked in the hotel business before becoming a professor of religion at the same Michigan college.

Claudine's dinner was a multicourse, traditional French meal consisting of many of her personal specialties. Everything was excellent. She served it all on her best China with cute silverware holders to keep your utensils off the tablecloth. The conversation and hospitality were even better than the food. She had been an Eatwith host for seven years and loved to meet people. The conversation never stopped. We heard about her travels and adventures in various parts of the world. She instructed us on French etiquette for how to cut various shaped cheeses. (The rules are complex, of course!) Everything flowed so smoothly it was 11:30 before anyone noticed the time. We thanked her and said our goodbyes. Last to leave, I described my mum flower debacle. She laughed hard and said she wouldn't have minded receiving mums. (But she did mention her sister would have been mortified!)

We headed down the Métro entrance around midnight. A man clearly pretending to be drunker than he was, fake stumbled toward Courtney reaching for her purse. She saw it coming a mile away and with cat-like quickness darted away from him. His efforts exposed; he ran off in the other direction. The years spent living in St. Louis paid off in city smarts. The Métro ride home was for sure a different crowd—a little rougher around the edges with drunk teenagers trading drinks from a bottle and loudly singing songs together. Despite the rowdy train car, it was all in good fun and still felt safe. We made it home without further incident, another full day under our belts.

9

BEFORE SUNSET...AND AFTER

After the late night, we slept longer than we would have preferred. First up on our agenda today was the Marché d'Aligre in the twelfth arrondissement. We rode the Métro to the busy Gare de Lyon about a five-minute walk from the market. In operation since the eighteenth century, Marché d'Aligre is one of the classic French markets. It has both an outdoor produce market and an adjacent covered section (Marché Beauvau) with artisanal meats, cheeses, and baked goods. Completing what many feel is the best market in Paris is another whole section, the Puces d'Aligre. This flea market sells antique items, ancient books, vintage jewelry and much more. Courtney and I love flea markets, in Europe in particular. We only had about an hour until the market closed, so we hurried through the stalls searching for hidden treasures. The next time we will definitely arrive sooner. Courtney bought several vintage items—a cameo, a one-of-a-kind metal bracelet, and some antique ice tongs. I picked out three other pieces of unique jewelry for her, but we had to pass on them telling the seller they were "trop cher" (too expensive). Insisting one piece was real silver, he wasn't interested in bargaining. We weren't so sure about the silver. We thanked him and wished him, "Bonne journée."

We walked about a block to a wine bar targeted in my research, Le Baron Rouge. It was better than advertised. They had an extensive wine list available in various sizes. The bartenders were approachable and appreciated our French. We ordered a "pot" (500ml) of a Rhone red and a large charcuterie plate, "Le Grand Mixte." The tables nearby were filled with locals who all seemed to know each other. It was obviously a jovial, post-market hangout. All around the bar, they had barrels of wine direct from wineries. You could get one liter (or larger) take-away containers of really good wine for ridiculously low prices. Planning to walk most of the afternoon, it wasn't practical to take any wine to go. We wished this cool spot was closer to our neighborhood. Deciding to use the bathrooms before our next adventure, I was pointed outside and down a back alley to an outhouse style shack. When I opened the door, I laughed out loud. I had found the first Turkish toilet of the trip! Courtney took a pass on the bathroom break...

Rue Crémieux is one of the cutest one-block neighborhoods in Paris. A short walk from the Le Baron Rouge toward the Seine, and we were there. The street calls to mind the famous "Rainbow Row" of Charleston, South Carolina with every house painted a different shade of pleasing pastel color. Some are decorated in trompe-l'oeil, and most have luscious landscaping in large terracotta pots. The narrow cobblestone street of quaint row houses transports you back to the late nineteenth century. While blogs often refer to it as a "secret" hidden gem in Paris, it isn't really that secret. At times, it was difficult to get a picture without someone in the background posing ridiculously, often right on the steps of someone else's house. The residents have actually (unsuccessfully) petitioned Paris to put up gates and close the street on evenings and weekends.

We walked a couple blocks into the heart of the Quinze-Vingts neighborhood. This neighborhood in the twelfth arrondissement is not a tourist destination but is quintessentially Parisian. "Quinze-Vingts" stands fifteen-twenties or three hundred. It was named for a famous hospital for the blind which had three hundred beds. The odd numeric term comes from the ancient vigesimal system (based on twenties) used by the Gauls, a Celtic people. When Rome conquered Gaul, the Celtic numbering system was hybridized with the Roman decimal system. In fact, the French word for eighty, "quatre-vingts" is a product of this hybridization. In any event, we loved the Quinze-Vingts neighborhood for being so normal. The vibe is laid back with normal folks just going about their business. We found a nice-looking café at a crossing, Café Quai 33, and sat down for some caffeine and hydration before heading to our next destination.

The Coulée Verte was one of our very favorite places in all of Paris—a romantic hideaway featured in the poignant 2004 film, *Before Sunset*, starring Ethan Hawke and Julie Delpy. Also known as the Promenade Plantée, the path started its life an elevated railway line in 1859. This line ceased operation in 1969. In the 1980s, the area started to revitalize. The abandoned, elevated path was reclaimed and repurposed by an architect and landscape artist to create one of the "true" hidden gems of Paris. Open since 1993, this free 4.5 kilometer stretch of park is an absolute delight. You can access the beginning of the path via a staircase at 12 Avenue Daumesnil.

As you top the staircase, you enter a little piece of heaven in the midst of bustling Paris. The landscaping is remarkable in that it feels at once both beautifully manicured and yet still a little wild. The path is segmented, and you pass seamlessly from one scene to another, each a little different with reflecting pools, benches, and arched passageways. The smell of jasmine floats on the breeze. Roses, climbing plants, luscious garden beds, and lime and hazelnut trees are found in abundance. Copious shade cools on a warm day. All along the path are views of notable buildings of a variety of architectural styles. At one point, the path actually passes directly through a modern curved building which arcs around it on either side.

The beauty is undeniable, but it is more than that; it is the mood and the feeling of the place. The Coulée Verte is the ultimate place to "flaneur," a lovely French word which means to wander aimlessly simply for pleasure's sake. You experience an incredible cross section of Parisian culture: young and old—strollers and canes, unsupervised school-aged kids walking (or running) through the park, dogs, lots of dogs, high school and college students, young professionals, and the working class—all of ethnic and racial diversity and all showing respect with a smile, a nod or a bonjour. Everyone we asked was happy to take our picture and wanted to make sure the shots were perfect before moving on. Everywhere along the path people, young and old, were holding hands, stealing a kiss, or even going in for a passionate one. At one point, the platform widens with an ice cream stand and fun activities for kids. I am not sure, but I think I even remember a small carrousel… of course there was, this is Paris. Later, a large park spreads out widely around the path with Le Jardin Reuilly-Paul Pernin to one side and Square Eugène Thomas on the opposite. The lawns were filled with people lounging in the sun, picnicking, and drinking wine. Toward the end of our walk, the surroundings became more working class with several immigrant communities living side by side but felt no less charming and just as safe. We were sad to exit the Coulée Verte, but it was time to hit the road and hop the Métro home to get ready for yet another trip highlight.

Our big splurge for Paris was the highly rated restaurant, Boutary (rated number five by one source). We knew it was going to be the most expensive meal of the trip but figured it would be an unforgettable experience. We freshened up at our place and put on our fanciest clothes, me in my sports jacket for the one and only time of the trip. We went out early to participate in the evening apéro custom. After failing to find a seat at a couple different bars, we snagged a terrace table at "Le Petit Buci." The bar sits at one of the major corners of Rue de Buci, a happening little strip of cafés and restaurants. Greeting and ordering all in French, we were served with a smile—a Ricard for me and a white sangria for Courtney. The people watching was great with fashion running the gambit from causal to hip, and all the way to suits and evening gowns. Tourist garb stuck out like a sore thumb, and we played one of our favorite games, "Guess the Country?"

Arriving at Boutary, we were taken to the elegantly decorated upstairs dining room with an ultra-modern lighted flare pattern carried through the tables, floor, and walls. The design artist added contrasting, classical fixtures which lit the room as the sun went down outside the opened shutters. Our waiter was energetic and funny but dead serious about his profession. We hit it off right away when we asked for the French menu. He asked if we wanted to speak in English or French during the meal; we chose the latter. Later in the meal, when we would break into English to ask a question, he would playfully scold us insisting we continue in French while coaching us on our vocabulary. This was a great exercise in improving our French. The downside was that when he explained each complex and exquisite dish, he did so in rapid-fire French. When we got home from this extraordinary meal, Courtney and I sat together and tried to take notes from memory to capture all the details of the seven-course tasting menu with caviar and paired wines. The dishes were not described anywhere on the menu. The courses were chosen at the pleasure of the chef who crafted artistic masterpieces from the freshest and most unusual ingredients. Apologies to the chef, I am certain our memories left out many amazing details.

Our waiter arrived at our table with our first wine, a bright, crisp Riesling designed to open the palate. Before our first culinary experience, our waiter gave us a lesson on caviar. He explained the restaurant had strict specifications for their caviar. They only served caviar from sturgeon of a specific size, caught only at precise locations, at particular depths, and only during certain seasons. Then, he explained how choices made during processing and aging impacted taste. The chef prefers to have his caviar salted less than some and aged for eight to ten months. The longer aging with less salt leads to buttery and creamy undertones (with less of the harsh salty taste I associated with caviar from the few times I've had it before). He suggested we try eating it the traditional way, served directly on the back of your hand, tasting a few eggs at a time letting the flavors roll around on the palate. Eating it this way evolved for safety reasons. Historically, if the caviar irritated the skin, it was poisoned and should not be consumed. He then applied a large glob of caviar to the back of each of our hands and left us to enjoy. The taste first exploded into your mouth then softened to indeed give a buttery deliciousness. Savoring each little taste slowly, me with eyes closed emitting involuntary, audible happy sighs, our dinner was off to a great start.

The courses now proceeded with our waiter presenting each with great flare along with a detailed description of the high-quality, artisanal ingredients mixed together in surprising, delectable combinations. First was a small corn chip bowl filled with beans of summer, corn, and an edible purple flower. It looked too pretty to eat. Next came a plate with two offerings— short bread with tapenade, and pickled anchovy and lemon paired with a gnarled bean chip topped with an unusual mushroom and caramelized shallots. Following that combination came an absolute work of art—delicate pieces of smoked salmon with passion fruit, mangos, pureed sweet potatoes, special spicy greens, pickled red onion, sea asparagus, and a mind-blowing sauce beyond description. We moved on to our second wine, a Northern Rhone white from Saint-Joseph with powerful flavors and honey undertones.

With each course, one of us would exclaim, "This is one of the best things I have ever eaten," only to repeat it with the next presentation. This brings me to the absolute best dish of the trip. The waiter arrived with two covered round bowls. I said, "It looks like you have a surprise." He smiled and said something like, "Oh you just wait!" There was already an enchanting smell in the air. After setting a bowl in front of each of us, he dramatically removed the covers. We were immediately engulfed by a heavenly smoke. While the smoke cleared, he explained that the large mound of caviar on top had been cherry wood smoked. The base of the dish was a special kind of French potato pureed with chives and pressed into a cylindrical mold. The potatoes had been cooked in what is considered the best butter in France made by the renowned Monsieur Bordier from Brittany (his process takes twelve times longer than most commercial butters allowing it to mature, deepening in flavor and complexity). In between the caviar and the puréed potatoes was a crisp, feathery ultra-thin potato chip. The base of the dish contained a thick, buttery white sauce. I would hazard to say this may be the most delicious thing I have ever put in my mouth!

However, we were not even close to being done. Following the smoked caviar came one of the most unusual dishes, tender chunks of asparagus with wild garlic ice cream (think fantastic!) in a French cheese sauce with flaky pink chips of some sort and pennywort stems and leaves. Next was the fish course, a delicate monkfish which favored lobster, topped with a Japanese miso, honey mustard sauce along with mini turnips and sweet peas. Moving from white to red, our next glass was a Saint-Émillion that was outstanding. This paired nicely with the meat course— rare filet of duck with a green pea purée and morel mushrooms. It was sprinkled with dabs of rhubarb and cashew bits and bathed in a famous French sauce whose recipe dates to the Middle Ages.

Finally, we got to the desserts, plural! The palate cleanser, pre-dessert was freaking out of this world by itself—rhubarb and grapefruit compote with a dill whipped cream topped with an edible flower. Courtney chose for her main dessert fresh strawberries with fromage frais (a soft, fresh sweet cheese) in strawberry vinegar with basil ice cream. I went with a 90 percent pure hardened chocolate ball covered with crème fraiche then dusted with cocoa powder and cardamom. We were fully sated… Then came coffee with post-dessert—almond cakes with pistachio cream along with a firm, mini chocolate cake topped with fondue and sprinkled with unknown savory toppings. The dinner may have cost more than a month's rent at our first apartment in 1989 but it was worth every penny!

On our way back home, we took a detour down the hidden passage-way, le Cour du Commerce Saint-Andre, near our place. You would have to be a local (or have done obsessive Google Maps study!) to know about this lane. We had walked down it earlier in the trip during apéro hour, and it was hopping. Most of the businesses were now closed save a couple restaurants serving their last customers. It was shadowy, dark, and oh so romantic. I grabbed Courtney and sneaked in a kiss in the deserted lane. After all this is Paris! Our second to last day in Paris was once again an action-packed day and maybe one of the best of the trip—Marché d'Aligre, the Coulée Verte, an apéro and one of the best meals of our life.

10

A DREAM FULFILLED

On our last day in Paris, we slept to a reasonable time and set out on a "flex" day. We decided to start the day walking parts of our neighborhood, Saint-Germain-des-Prés, which we had not yet seen. Courtney was on a mission to buy macarons and chocolates from some of the famous named stores. We stopped in Pierre Hermé on Blvd. Saint-Germain for macarons. We bought a tin of seven, dropping a significant chunk of change to do so. Courtney had been reading about chocolate shops competing for the honor of being called the best. We walked a few blocks to the highly rated À La Mère de Famille. The attendant there was a sweet woman who was intrigued by our French. She wanted to know where we were from and commented that Americans usually don't try to speak much French. We talked about how the "R" sound in French was really hard for Americans and she agreed. We bought some individual pieces along with a small and large box of chocolates (the small one to give as a gift later in the trip). As we were leaving, she winked at us and asked if we'd like a couple chocolates for the road.

We decided to make one last trek to Luxembourg Gardens. We passed through the book market in the square outside Saint-Sulpice to get there. We found a bench near the reflecting pool and ate our individual (and free) pieces of chocolate. We said a sad goodbye to the gardens and vowed to return. We picked up part of the Green Guide tour of Saint-Germain in what was described as a "lively" neighborhood though it wasn't very lively in late morning. We did run into a shoe store along the way… and well, you know the rest of the story. I was soon the proud owner of another pair of women's shoes.

We made a quick visit to the striking Romanesque church, Église Saint-Germain-des-Prés, the oldest standing church in Paris. It was built in the eleventh century on the site of an abbey founded in 543. Saint-Germanus (496-576), one of the first bishops of Paris is believed to be buried here. In 886, the building was devastated by Viking invaders. It was renovated in 1000 and has been added to over the years. The colorful interior is gorgeous and awe inspiring. Outside there is a small courtyard with a bronze Picasso sculpture. We walked up to Rue Jacob and back to Rue de Buci. We decided on ice cream for lunch—one of our favorite vacation meals. On Rue de Buci, I finally had Berthillon's ice cream from a streetside stand—chocolate and rhum raison (which was called Créole in French). Court chose the Amarino shop and went with three fruity flavors with a macaron on top. I hate to tell you this Paris, but Nice and Florence definitely have you beat in gelato.

We popped back to our place to do the bulk of our packing before our early morning departure the next day. After feeling settled, we rode the Métro to the Arc de Triomphe and the Champs-Élysées. The Arc is definitely spectacular, but the crowds jostling for selfies reminded us of the Leaning Tower of Pisa. We ended up glad we didn't stand in line with the tourist horde to go to the top. It was cool to see the multi-lane roundabout and the traffic chaos that has made its way into so many iconic movies. To our disappointment, the Champs-Élysées was a high-end tourist trap. Luxury stores with ostentatious facades had long lines to enter. There was a humorous but somewhat embarrassing display of American businesses—McDonald's, Nike, Disney, Levi's and Five Guys. This is who they think we are and... maybe they are right?

We made it to the end of the street reaching Place de la Concorde and the Luxor Obelisk. Previously named Place Louis XV, it became Place de la Revolution in 1792 where it was the site of the guillotining of Louis XVI, Marie-Antoinette, Danton, and Robespierre. It was hard to appreciate the history; the enormous square is a maze of traffic that makes you feel like you have entered a *Frogger* video game. The Luxor Obelisk is 3000 years old and one of a pair of carved stones which framed the portal of the Luxor temple during the reign of Ramesses II. It was gifted to France in 1830 by the ruler of Ottoman Egypt. The Obelisk had been coveted by France going back to Napoleon's campaign in Egypt in 1799.

Past Place de la Concorde, we reached the Jardin des Tuileries for the first time. It was filled with people, everyone enjoying the sunshine sitting in chairs and benches around fountains and reflecting pools. The gardens were elegant but the crushed gravel paths in the dry May heat left a layer of white dust everywhere. Exiting the Tuileries to the left, Courtney really wanted to try the famous "African" hot chocolate at Angelina's but with the heat and a long line, we skipped it and backtracked to Place Vendome. This enormous square is ringed by the most exclusive high-end shops and jewelry stores. The place was initially created by Louis XIV to commemorate the glory of his grand armies. An equestrian statue of Louis XIV originally adorned the center of the square though it was destroyed during the French revolution. The current column was started in 1806 at the command of Napoleon to celebrate his victory at Austerlitz. It was modeled after Trajan's column and depicts Napoleon as a Roman conqueror. Its bronze plates are said to have been created from cannons taken in battle. The statue and column were eventually pulled down. After the Paris Commune, it was rebuilt with Napoleon restored to all his glory atop the column. It is a glamorous square where window shopping is the best we could do.

It was mid-afternoon, and we were now hungry after nothing but chocolates and ice cream for lunch. One of my targeted "joints" was the Happy Café along Rue de Rivoli. This crêpe place was highly rated for friendliness and tasty, cheap eats. Courtney grabbed a terrace table under an awning while I ordered two crêpes and coffees despite the heat. Nine days in Paris was catching up to us. I was asked if I wanted the order "sur place" (to eat there) or for "emporter" (take-away); the prices for each were different. I answered we were eating "sur place." The crêpes were fabulous and with the coffee, we had a new lease on life. I went back in to pay. The owner could not remember what we had ordered. I repeated our order in my best, and now much faster, French. A French mother and daughter were in line close to me. The French woman spoke across the counter to the owner saying, "Look at this American speaking French." She then looked at me pointedly and said, "Vous comprenez?" (Do you understand?) I responded, "Oui, je parle un peu de français," with a smile. She answered with a nod and said in English, "It is really nice to go to a foreign country and speak their language, isn't it?" I had to agree.

After our respite, we crossed the Tuileries and then the Seine on a quest to find "La Grande Épicerie," a kind of Whole Foods on steroids and one of Ina Garten's favorite places in Paris. On our way, we ran into the luxury department store, Le Bon Marché; it is interesting to me that one of the priciest stores in Paris is called "The Good Deal" or "inexpensive." Depending on the brand, the prices were jaw dropping. Courtney found a straw bag she loved, but the floor model was blemished. The price for the bag was not outrageous. We asked the clerk in the department if they had another. They did not, so Court passed on it to continue her straw bag quest later.

A block down the road, we found La Grande Épicerie. The grocery store was awesome but overwhelming. It took us a little time to get our bearings. We wanted to buy picnic food for our last night—an evening trip to the Eiffel Tower. We ended up with a baguette, four cheeses, ham, artichoke dip, and mixed, fresh vegetables. We still had a bottle of wine left from La Dernière Goutte. We couldn't find French pickles (a favorite of Courtney's for their unusual taste, maybe more coriander?). I asked the girl at the welcome desk. She nodded and proceeded to walk me all the way across the store to point them out. We did our best not to hold up the check-out process with twelve cashiers serving one line. They, like everyone else in Paris, were very patient with our fumbled attempts to be efficient.

We walked twenty minutes home to meet our host for check-out; we were leaving early the next morning. She was tense and a little irritable. The place was a bit messy since we were in the midst of packing. We hadn't realized there was a dishwasher in the unit until the night before, and because of that, had only run one load. When she saw it was locked with a red blinking light, she became accusatory like I had broken it. The dishwasher seemed to have a delay and opened after a minute with no harm done. It was not a pleasant interaction and was surprising given her VRBO reviews. I wouldn't stay with her again. We mentioned we were going to the Eiffel Tower for sunset, and she responded, "Why would you do that??? It is too crowded and not safe!"

Not to be dissuaded, we rode the Métro to the Champ de Mars, the Left Bank greenspace flowing out from the tower. It was a younger crowd and a little rough around the edges but still felt safe. Everyone was having fun, mostly drinking wine and smoking the ubiquitous Parisian cigarettes. Hawkers circulated through the crowd pushing bottles of cold wine and beer. We had our food and drink in Courtney's backpack complete with the picnic blanket we bought in Nice on our first trip to France. We laid out our feast and opened our wine in full view of the tower. In a funny twist, Spanish soccer fans were in town for the Champion's League final and were dancing to Latin Pop blasting from portable speakers. Waiting for the Eiffel Tower to illuminate with nearby pulsating Latin beats felt odd and a little dissonant. The next day, the match against an English team at the Stade de France turned into chaos. English fans who had been sold a large number of false tickets began to storm the gates and jump the fences. French authorities used force—tear gas and pepper spray. The fallout from the mess reached the highest levels of the French government and dominated the news for the next couple weeks.

Despite the Spanish pop, the night at the Eiffel Tower was a joyful experience. We asked a couple girls sitting behind us to take our picture in front of the tower. They turned out to be American students in Paris who said they were jealous of our picnic spread. With the sun setting behind the tower, it was an absolutely surreal scene. It was a pinch yourself, "Am I really here?" moment. When the Eiffel Tower started to sparkle, it further transformed the truly magical scene. It took Courtney and me right back to eighth grade French class with a dream to one day visit Paris. Anyone who has ever been to Paris will tell you how special it is, and we are no different. But, having met in a French class exactly forty years prior, our time here was more than special.

11

GASCONY, JE T'AIME

Our next destination was rural Gascony, an area renowned for the musketeers, duck, and, in my mind, especially for Armagnac. I had pushed to add Gascony to our itinerary in order to visit Armagnac distilleries. In my first book, I spent a whole chapter describing Armagnac and its obvious superiority to its more well-known cousin, Cognac, so I won't repeat it here (most of my friends and family are already tired of me going on about it anyway). Gascony is known for slow tourism and is the polar opposite of frenetic Paris. I was worried Courtney would be bored with the jarring change of pace and my hyper-focus on Armagnac. I ended up being quite wrong.

Leaving Paris early in the morning on the TGV high-speed train, we decided to schedule an Uber rather than rely on the Métro to reach Gare Montparnasse. We arrived in time to have coffee before boarding a half hour ahead of departure. For the first leg of our journey, we were the only people in our first-class car. We raced along at 200+ mph making a couple stops before rolling into Poitiers. I had hoped for more sweeping views of the countryside, but there were often earthen walls built up around the track, I suppose to limit the noise. In Poitiers, we had an hour layover before our next train to Bordeaux.

Poitiers is a town famous in the history of France for two major battles fought here. In 732, Charles Martel stopped the advance of the Moorish invasion. Then in 1356, it saw one of the most significant battles of the Hundred Years' War. The Black Prince carried the day defeating and capturing King John II of France. The battle ended the first phase of the Hundred Years' War and led to the Treaty of Brétigny. In the agreement, the French ceded most of southwest France to England in exchange for the King of England renouncing his claim to the French throne. King John of France was held prisoner and eventually gave his two sons as hostages in his place. The historic district in Poitiers is reported to be picturesque and worth visiting—the district around the train station, not so much...

The station was in an edgy neighborhood, and everything in the place seemed to be broken. With my pain flaring and a broken elevator, we chose to remain in the hallway near the platforms rather than carrying our heavy suitcases down to the main station. Needing the bathroom, I walked around to a set of escalators, also broken. Walking down the escalator stairs, I found two unisex bathrooms at the extreme opposite end of the terminal. There was a long line waiting to use them. When my turn came, there was no toilet seat or paper, and the bathroom was filthy. As with Turkish toilets, Courtney chose to skip this one. Without any place to sit, the hour passed slowly. It probably isn't fair to Poitiers, but we left without a great impression. Eventually we were relieved to be back in first class and on our way to Bordeaux. The trip to Bordeaux was uneventful. The first-class car was nearly full this time. Like restaurants, we were struck by how quiet it was.

At the station in Bordeaux, we were able to quickly rent our car with only one brief misstep, going to the wrong parking garage. We were offered a diesel Fiat 500X which definitely saved on gas. The little car had some get up and go which was an added bonus. Exiting Bordeaux, we passed through the town of Cadaujac. We breezed past a restaurant with a terrace full of people. I realized it was already 1:30pm. Knowing that French restaurants shut down around two, we made a U-turn and hurried back to the restaurant. The waitress looked a little stressed when we asked for a table so late in the lunch "hour" but nodded toward an empty space on the terrasse. I do have to say it was the fastest served meal we ate in France! This was fine with us since we were excited to get to Gascony. The food was very good for an improvised choice. Courtney's "Locals Vote with Their Feet" theory held true again. I had water since I was driving, but Courtney had a glass of excellent, A.O.C., Pessac-Leognan wine, which was from the region in Bordeaux where we happened to be.

We drove through the département (French state) of the Landes. In the eighteenth century, Landes was a sparsely populated, marshy area until the French undertook stabilizing the wet, mobile sand dunes of the nearby coast. As the area of the Landes dried out, Napoleon III began a huge project planting pine forests to fix the soil in place. Driving through the area, it was scrubby pines as far as the eye could see with large piles of cut wood along the road. Our host Jean later explained, not much else grows in the sandy soil here. Lumber is the main industry. We passed from the Landes to the département of the Gers (pronounced "jhair" or "jhairs" depending on the speaker), the heart of Gascony. The change in the landscape was dramatic. Rolling, rural farmland and wide-open vistas reminded both of us of Nebraska where we grew up. What Nebraska doesn't have much of is vineyards (or castles). When we saw the first vines that would soon become my treasured spirit, Armagnac, we stopped and pulled down a dirt road to snap some pictures. Speeding down one lane, two-way roads, we were the only car in sight for most of the remaining journey.

Les Bruhasses is yet another place words cannot do justice. Searching through endless rental properties, I stumbled across its website the summer before. The pictures and reviews looked too good to be true.

Reviewers all agreed; it was one of the best places they had stayed in the whole world. The gorgeous, bucolic setting was only topped by the unbelievable hospitality, the reviews went. With reservations at a place with such rave reviews, I hoped our expectations were not so high that we'd end up disappointed. Turning onto the rutted dirt road which gave way to the manor house, it was clear they weren't high enough! We arrived about 5pm and pulled around to the crushed gravel parking area which had numbered signs. Not knowing which one to choose, I parked in one and stepped out of the car to find a man with a jolly smile hopping off a riding lawn mower. He was Jean, the French-Canadian husband of the couple who ran the bed-and-breakfast. Jean greeted us like long-lost friends. After introductions, I asked which numbered spot I should park in. He laughed and said it didn't matter. The signs were only there to keep "the French" from double parking. He directed us to see Hélène for check-in at the front of the extraordinary manor home, two symmetric towers at either end. He jumped back on the mower and waved, saying he would see us later.

Hélène greeted us with the same enthusiasm and showed us around the home and grounds before taking us to our suite. The front of the home was lined with umbrellaed tables and chaise lounges which looked onto Jean's resplendent row of roses and immaculate landscaping. Just inside there was a large, ornate dining room, big enough to seat all the guests at once. Fresh cooked breakfast was served here each morning. Toward the back, there was a room for the guests with a refrigerator, cold drinks, silverware and everything you might need for a picnic on the back terrace. The back terrace looked out onto a unique little building we later learned was at one time a pigeonnerie, a sign of wealth centuries ago. Bushes and towering trees, many leaning at artistic angles, ringed the boundary of the property. Gorgeous and bucolic indeed it was.

Hélène took us to our suite, "Hymne au Soleil," the left tower of the grand home. The first floor of our suite had a large modern bathroom and living area with a view onto the back terrace and grounds.

A curving staircase led to a bedroom and desk area. It was spacious and spotless. Everything was tastefully decorated in a style befitting an eighteenth-century manor house. As Courtney and I looked at each other with awe, Hélène reminded us that every evening at 6:30, they hosted an apéro hour for the guests on the front terrace. She served wines from her family's fifth-generation winery/Armagnac distillery located twenty minutes away. After a long day of travel, freshening up and sitting down with a glass of wine in a peaceful setting sounded perfect!

Happy hour on the terrasse was splendid. Hélène's family wine was very good, and the experience was quite relaxing. We got to meet the other guests who were of a variety of nationalities. Not having stayed in many bed-and-breakfasts before, we found it interesting to get to know our fellow travelers and hear about their adventures in France and beyond. I didn't necessarily jibe with everyone around the table, which was fine, but as a psychiatrist, I enjoyed watching the dynamics of the conversation, trying to figure people out.

Over the course of our stay, we met lovely couples from Paris, San Francisco, Toulouse and one from Australia (though the wife really wanted us to know she spoke fluent French). We met a real character—Mike, a fellow Armagnac connoisseur, and his wife who had places in both San Diego and Colorado (more on Mike later). We met a couple of interesting and engaging guides for a group walking the famous Camino de Santiago which passes close by. A night or two later, we met some of the group they were guiding including a verbose, hubristic woman from Alexandria very proud of her spirituality and a couple from Idaho who only seemed capable of complaining. I felt sorry for their guides. Finally, Hélène and Jean had two close friends coming in from Singapore for a personal visit. Both charming and sophisticated, we enjoyed talking with them during the stay. They were actually looking to move to the area. After traveling extensively, they explained that unspoiled, authentic Gascony was one of their favorite places in the world.

After our hectic agenda in Paris, I had purposefully under planned

Gascony. I had only made one reservation for the four days (at an Armagnac distillery). Hélène approached us to talk about our plans for the stay. She explained the Armagnac houses would be closed the following day, Sunday, but she would give us some suggestions on things to do. She then asked if we had dinner plans or reservations for the night. I had done research on a few targeted restaurants (of course) and mentioned two at the top of my list. I asked if we might be able get into one of them. Given it was now close to 7pm, she frowned like it was unlikely but offered to make calls on our behalf. She came back and nodded with a smile. She had procured the last table for us at the restaurant in Larressingle—so long as we didn't mind leaving soon.

We hurried to Larressingle on a winding road which at times was no more than a tiny alley slicing through thick vegetation. A couple times when Google Maps told me to turn, I looked at Courtney and exclaimed, "really?" squinting for the tiniest of openings to the left or right. The staff must have been alerted to our pending arrival. Everyone seemed to be checking us out as we approached L'Auberge de Larressingle. A waitress greeted us and led us to a table overlooking the castle a mere one hundred meters away. Larressingle is the smallest fortified village in France (a circumference of just 270 meters) and is nicknamed "Little Carcassonne." It one of Les Plus Beaux Village de France, a list of "The Most Beautiful Villages of France" named not only for being idyllic rural towns but also for cultural significance. The church was built in the twelfth century before the town was fortified in the thirteenth. Very few people live inside the village now, and Hélène had joked that the town's population recently doubled when a family of five moved in. With the late evening sun at an angle, the aged, light stone walls sparkled in splendor. It was clear we were in for a special dinner.

We started with an apéritif. Courtney had Floc de Gascogne, a sweet mixture of one-third Armagnac and two-thirds grape juice. I learned something in ordering from the apéritif menu. The waitress explained in French (of note, few if any in the area speak much English) that young

Armagnac with an ice cube is commonly served before meals, and the older Armagnacs are reserved for sipping as digestifs. For my starter, I had a puff pastry filled with warm Cabécou cheese served with a small salad garnished with white beans, apple slices and radishes. Courtney began with the "Plate of Gascony"—smoked duck breast, confit of duck gizzards, and duck foie gras on a slice of bread with local walnuts served around a few leaves of lettuce. It was billed as a salad but was definitely more duck than salad! Both the apéritifs and starters were outstanding. With the sun dropping, the colors of the castle walls darkened and deepened.

With our meal, we ordered a bottle of a local red, Côtes de Gascogne—something we can't find in North Carolina. We really came to love the rustic, inexpensive, and undiscovered wines of the region. My main dish was perfectly done duck breast while Courtney went with a tender piece of veal. Both were served with marinated local vegetables and a crusty mound of potatoes. Now with the sun really starting to set, the darker tones in the stone of the castle now glowed almost orange. Dessert for Courtney was to become one of her trip favorites and a local specialty, apple croustade—think of the most incredible apple pie you can imagine baked on delicate French pastry stretched thin and topped with artistic flourishes of the left-over feathery pasty bits. When I have a choice, I almost always go chocolate. I had profiteroles bathed in a thick chocolate sauce with salted butter and caramel ice cream. With a drive home in the dark, we passed on digestifs and chose instead a walk through the castle.

Walking around to the entrance of the walled village, twilight had descended. This is one of Courtney's favorite parts of the day—still light enough to see but with an eerie purple dimness. We passed the ancient stone bridge over the now empty moat and entered a fairy tale. The entire place was deserted. There were a smattering of yellow lights casting enchanting shadows as we walked hand in hand. It was easy to close our eyes and imagine living in the Middle Ages. We did a slow meander around the circular town, peaking around corners and down ancient wells. Passing one of the lights, our shadows were cast long in front of us holding hands, and I was able to capture two of my favorite pictures of us ever. We did run into two people within the village walls sitting on a staircase talking. We greeted them courteously and continued on our walk. Driving home in the dark was an adventure. Was it possible the roads had grown even more narrow over dinner? Five hours after arriving in Gascony, pulling back into Les Bruhasses lit up against the night in its own magical way, I was already falling in love.

12

MEDIEVAL NIGHTS, TAKE TWO

A fter Paris, it was a joy to sleep in. We were the last guests to join the breakfast table. Hélène promptly came round to ask our preference for coffee or tea and if we took sugar or cream. Black coffee and lots of it was our answer with a smile. We were served Jean's famous Canadian "French Toast" with maple syrup, yogurt, and orange juice. There was a basket of croissants and bread along with a selection of three homemade jams. They were all delicious, but one stood out. Hélène explained her secret recipe complete with pictures. During the winter months, distillation of Armagnac from local white wine takes place in the cellars or "chai" (pronounced "shay"). The distillation process takes several days while the continuous alembic still slowly produces, on average, two to four barrels of clear eau de vie per day. At the start of the distillation season, large parties are held in the cellars where friends and family are invited to celebrate the product of their labor. One tradition is filling a large canning pot with fruits of the season and fresh-off-the-still eau de vie. Once heated, the pot is set on fire, and eventually everyone has a warm glass to drink around the wood-fired still. Hélène takes the liquor-soaked fruits left at the end of the process and uses them to make the jam.

As breakfast came to a close, Hélène came around to advise each couple on their plan for their day, keeping in mind their particular interests. My research had focused on towns to the west of Les Bruhasses (the direction of most of the Armagnac production). Given it was Sunday, she suggested touring a number of towns to the east. After her help with dinner the night before, I told her I was planning to do anything she recommended (a phrase I repeated several times during the stay). She reassured me we would get to visit several Armagnac houses on Monday and Tuesday. She pulled out a pre-printed map and began to circle in red about twelve notable villages of interest to the east, describing each in detail. In her description, she mentioned a local cocktail called Pousse Rapière. It is a drink which contains a liqueur made from a closely guarded recipe of Armagnac and bitter orange liqueur. This liqueur is then mixed with Vin Sauvage, a local sparkling wine. One of the towns she suggested, St. Puy, was the only place where the liqueur was made. Before starting our tour, she suggested we first drive about five minutes up the road to the closest town of Condom where we could find a market. Given much was closed on Sundays and Mondays, planning a picnic on the back terrace for one of those nights was a good plan.

Sunday is not Condom's big market day, but there were a handful of stands open. The produce looked fresh and inviting. We ended up with cucumbers, ancienne tomatoes, cherries, apricots, and strawberries. Everyone throughout the market was very pleasant, but we got a lot of curious, "You're not from here," looks. In many places in Gascony, Americans seem to be a bit of a novelty. At one stand, I owed 3.80 euros. I pulled out a ten-euro bill. While the woman stared at the ten fumbling with change, I realized she would have preferred a smaller bill, and I quickly rifled through my wallet for what I thought was a five. When she handed me 40+ euros in change, I was confused. Courtney pointed out I had mistakenly given her a fifty. I apologized profusely and tried to give her a five instead, but she waved me off with a laugh. Next, we went about a block down to a boulangerie to pick up some bread. While debating which of the many loaves to buy, a man came out with a many-layered cake which he placed on a display table next to three others. We commented on how beautiful they were. Stopping to talk to us, he explained it was Mothers' Day in France, and these were typical cakes for the occasion. On our way back to drop off the food, we talked about how everyone in Gascony, from the restaurant the night before to the market and boulangerie today, had been so friendly.

Before heading east, we plotted a path for seeing a few of the twelve villages Hélène had described. Remembering St. Puy was known for the Puisse Rapière, I proposed starting there, then making a circuit of the other recommended towns close to it. Approaching the quaint village at the top of a steep hill, it appeared deserted. We parked near the church and got out of the car to a very hot day. As it was almost noon, I checked my phone for restaurants open on Sunday. Only one appeared to be operating in town. With my hip hurting again, we walked a couple painful blocks and approached the restaurant's large terrace which was completely empty. Feeling confident we could procure a table, I walked up to the wait staff and asked for a table for two. They answered they were "Complet" (full). I looked around curiously and repeated, "Complet?" "Oui," they stated definitively. We decided to walk back and see the church, but unlike churches almost everywhere else we had been, it was closed and locked. Near the restaurant, there had been a sign pointing toward a château. I made the case to walk back in that direction to at least see something in the town. We passed the restaurant which, by then, did have a sizeable group seated but was not yet full. We turned left toward the château and faced a steep hill. Halfway up, sweating in full sun, stabbing pain with each step, I surrendered and suggested we go back to the car and drive up. Approaching by car, we noticed the gates of the château were closed and despite trying side streets, we couldn't even get a good long view of it. St. Puy is definitely a cute town, but it wasn't a very good start to our tour.

Eric Kirchmann

Heading next for the village of Saint-Orens-Pouy-Petit, we found ourselves on country roads with vistas of neatly manicured farmland as far as the eye could see. We once again felt like we could have been in Nebraska. It felt like home. We even stopped a couple times to take pictures of views that resembled my grandfather's ranch. We parked outside the walls of Saint-Orens-Pouy-Petit which appeared to be hosting a town-wide garage sale. This picturesque village has fortifications dating to the thirteenth century. As the name suggests, the town was created from two separate parts. Saint-Orens was founded by the bishop of Agen, and Pouy Petit was a castle belonging to the Count of Gaure. Obviously not a big tourist site, we found it charming for its normal, everyday authenticity.

Walking down main street, we were indeed in the middle of a large garage sale. We wandered stand to stand receiving cordial greetings all the way. I was focused on looking for a restaurant or cafe where I could find a Pousse Rapière. Courtney was focused on shopping. She was drawn to a stand with two ladies sitting behind a couple tables with little girl dresses hanging from a rack. We lingered a little before walking on to check out the rest of the stands. At the end of the street stood the castle and the church. Neither was open. Around the side of the church, at the crest of the hill, were magnificent views of the countryside below. There was a food stand selling grilled sausages, cold drinks, and wine but no Pousse Rapière (or ice cream!). Wine was one euro, and the sausages looked good. We should have stopped to eat but did not.

We walked back through town and stopped at the tables with the little girl dresses. All in French, Courtney struck up what turned out to be a lovely conversation with a grandmother delighted to be passing on the cute (and very French) dresses from her granddaughter to ours in America. The price was four euros for one or ten euros for four. She meticulously went through the rack discussing sizes and pointing out the cutest ones. Courtney picked out four. Court also liked two trivets, and I explained we'd also like to buy them. The communication was tough with accents different here, but the second lady explained the adjoining tables were separate. They were just good friends who sat together. So, I turned to her to buy the trivets which were 0.50 euro each. She threw in two wine coasters for free. We wished them a good day and said our goodbyes. As we left, it was clear all four of us had enjoyed the heart-warming interaction.

We continued our journey venturing to Blaziert, ranked "fourth in Flowers" in France according to a quick check of the internet. This proved to be true in this small but lovely village. Entering the town, we ducked into the dark and quiet church of St Blaise. We were the only ones there. It was simple but pretty. Like most churches in the area, it proved to be the coolest part of town owing to its thick walls. Reading about it on my phone, I poked Courtney and pointed to a side room in the back right. There we found a charcoal drawing of Christ on the cross from an artist "practicing" for a larger canvas—a baptismal background from the fifteenth century. Viewing the divine, austere drawing in the hidden back room felt special, our little secret. We proceeded down the main street and took a left on the other main artery, a variety of brilliant flowers decorating nearly every surface. We detoured down an alley to find an ancient sundial built into an ancient wall. Like in Saint-Orens, at the edge of town, there were commanding views of the Ténarèze portion of Gascony. Once again, no open cafes or restaurants were to be found. Despite this, Blaziert was well worth the quick visit.

Our last stop on today's tour was a gem. La Romieu is another of the Plus Beaux Villages de France with its collegiate church classified a World Heritage Site by UNESCO. There were also gardens nearby though they were closed that day. Not having researched the town, I didn't realize how much it had to offer. It was now 3pm, and I read the church would be closing at four. I went inside and asked the docent if there was still time to see the church. She was very nice and explained we could pull it off if we hurried. She suggested we start by climbing the imposing tower and exploring the far end of the church working backwards. The sanctuary, she explained, would be closing early for a community concert (which she invited us to stay for). It was an engaging back and forth all in French. We were given audio guides which were very informative.

In 1062, two pilgrim monks from Rome stopped here on their way to Saint-Jacques de Compostelle. They founded a priory and a hospital here, a place of asylum for pilgrims traveling on the oft dangerous road. The Gascons referred to the monks as "Roumious" for "pilgrims of Rome" which eventually led to the name of the village. In 1312, a relative to the Pope born in La Romieu, was named cardinal. Cardinal d'Aux ordered the construction of the Collegial de La Romieu and abbey. This dignified Gothic structure was completed in 1318. It was ransacked in the sixteenth century during the Wars of Religion. What does remain is gorgeous. The Gothic cloisters lead to a cavernous chapel with notable stained-glass windows. A double spiral staircase climbs the 108-foot bell tower which provides stunning panoramic views of the area. Fourteenth century frescos were discovered on the vaulted sacristy and have been painstakingly restored. We toured many amazing churches on this trip, and this one is definitely near the top of the list.

We had time to finish our tour before the community concert and opted for a snack and a drink instead, given we hadn't eaten anything since breakfast. We found an open café and did the Parisian thing by just sitting down to claim it. An older waiter came out and addressed us sternly like we had done something wrong. Maybe he was just testing us because he did let us keep our table. My quest for a Pousse Rapière had ended. The name Pousse Rapière comes from a historical reference to the musketeers. The rapier was their weapon of choice, and the name translates to the "rapier's push," supposedly the effect it has when one drinks it neat. I enjoyed the pleasing drink without feeling stabbed in the gut while Courtney sipped on a cold rosé in the afternoon heat. Just then, a door across the street opened with unusual music filling the square. Out came a man playing a boha, a Gascon folk instrument with pipes and a rectangular bag traditionally made from sheep stomach. Following him in single file was the choir marching solemnly to the chapel for the concert. It was a very cool sight. After they passed, we noticed several cat statues and took some pictures for our granddaughter, Cora, a cat lover. It wasn't until later that we understood the significance of the cats.

La Romieu is also nicknamed the "village of cats" after a legend from the Middle Ages. The story goes that a peasant girl named Angeline was born in 1338. She soon lost both her parents and was taken in by neighbors. She loved cats, and it was said wherever she walked, cats followed. Drought brought on a terrible famine that lasted from 1342 to 1344. The townspeople were reduced to eating every available animal. Angeline was distraught and sought permission to save two cats. Given all the tragedy already visited on Angeline, her adoptive parents consented. The drought eventually ended. Local farmers now bringing in great harvests had a new problem, rats. The two cats Angeline saved had produced kittens. Angeline revealed her secret by giving the village twenty kittens who then saved the town from rat infestation. In the 1990s, to honor this legend, an artist began to craft cat sculptures which now can be found all over the town. This cute medieval legend has actually become a tourist draw for the village.

Our plan had been to squeeze in a visit to the famous Abbaye de Flaran, but in a nod to slow tourism, we chose to return to our tower in Les Bruhasses for a quick nap and freshening up before apéro hour. The social time on the front terrasse was interesting; the crowd changed every night with people checking in and out. Tonight's event saw a particularly convivial crowd. Hélène introduced us to Mike and Beth from Colorado (by way of San Diego). Mike and I hit it off immediately over our shared love of Armagnac and my connections to both San Diego and Colorado. They were leaving the next day for Spain and had already toured a number of Armagnac houses purchasing several top shelf bottles. Mike and Beth were planning an early meal at their apartment behind the manor house, but he insisted he would be back with some of his Armagnac for me to taste. While he was gone, Hélène asked us if we would like reservations at a restaurant in Fourcès. We could then have the picnic from the market the next night for dinner. She and Jean were going earlier to the restaurant with their friends from Singapore. She offered to call the restaurant on our behalf. Of course, we said, "Yes!" She confirmed the spot but added the restaurant had asked that we not be late for the 8:30 reservation. Just then, Mike returned carrying four bottles of Armagnac and some glasses. He shared small tasting portions of each while gregariously describing each estate and vintage. By the time I thought to look at my watch, we were late!

Fourcès is a twenty-minute drive from Les Bruhasses. For some reason, Google Maps took us by backroads rather than the more direct route. I pushed as hard as I could to make up some time. We entered the circle of the unusual circular bastide town and ended our wild ride, parking at precisely 8:29. We waved at Jean, Hélène, and their friends across the restaurant as we sat down on the terrasse overlooking the picturesque circular "square." There were only a few tables of people. Hospitality at the restaurant, like nearly everywhere in Gascony, was very welcoming. The waitress went out of her way to compliment our French and ask where we were from. Another nearby table was obviously English given their accent. They spoke in rather condescending tones. They must have been staying nearby, because one at the table left and sneaked back with beers they held under the tablecloth when the wait staff was close by. Their reception was understandably not as warm.

Courtney was ready for something other than duck, and the Auberge de Fourcès actually had some vegetarian options. She started with a vegetable basket with artichoke cream, truffles, peppers, dried tomatoes, and raw vegetables followed by her main dish, tarte fine with seasonal vegetables. Never mistaken for a vegetarian, I went steak tartare followed by confit de canard (duck preserved in its own fat then fried), foie gras salad, and duck breast and fries (done in duck fat). Can you sense a theme? Courtney's dessert was her favorite, apple croustade, this time served with a scoop of prune and Armagnac ice cream. I chose moelleux au chocolat with vanilla ice cream. Everything was exceptional. All had left now other than the two tables from Les Bruhasses. I watched Jean get up and chat with the owner and ask the waitress about her family. Jean and Hélène clearly cultivate relationships all over the area. We were the last to pay our bill, thanking the waitress for a wonderful experience.

Stepping down from the terrasse, we toured the town at night. The bastide town is arranged around a circular, arcaded center. Inside the circle is a lush greenspace with a central footpath framed by perfectly symmetric plane trees. The lighting at night enhanced the beauty. Around the arcade is a mix of ancient half-timbered and stone buildings. Walking around the circuit, I realized with embarrassment I had forgotten to tip. I hopped back up to the terrasse to talk with the waitress and hand her the pouboire. Returning to our walk, the history of the place felt powerful. We had sped into town over a fifteenth century bridge and after enjoying the "square," we walked a block or two up to the village's thirteenth century stone clock tower above an original gateway. It was hard to believe that for the second time in as many nights, we found ourselves alone in a medieval town. For the second night in a row, it was magical.

13

BUCKET LIST, PART ONE

reakfast today featured bread pudding made with Armagnac with
accompanying yogurt, coffee, croissants, and the special jams. It
was all delicious once again. We had a 2:30pm appointment with
Delord Armagnac which I had made a few weeks before the trip. I had
mentioned to Hélène earlier that we definitely wanted to visit her family's estate, Château de Millet. At breakfast, she let us know she had set up
a mid-morning visit with her sister, Laurence. Hélène expressed regret
that her father was out of town. I knew from my research that he was
quite a character based on the many five-star reviews of the Château de
Millet tour. Hélène mentioned her sister was quite busy running the estate but was making time to give us a tour and tasting. She suggested we
grab lunch afterwards in Éauze ("Ay-oh-z"), the capital of the Armagnac
region, before our afternoon appointment at Delord.

We drove about twenty minutes passing through Éauze to the nearby
Château de Millet. It was an idyllic setting with a neat grouping of buildings around the château which was set amongst the vines. Laurence
greeted us warmly and gave us a lesson in the history of Armagnac

and the estate itself. They had an interesting exhibit of see-through soil displays which illustrated the differences in terroir between Haut (limestone), Ténarèze (limestone and clay) and Bas Armagnac (sand and clay silt). In addition, there were educational displays, old Armagnac making artifacts, and an art gallery. The family is a passionate supporter of local artists. It was quite the renaissance setting. Laurence took us through a tasting of their many fines wines and Armagnacs. We felt bad for taking up too much of her time; she was clearly busy with her phone ringing off the hook. We ended up purchasing a red blend, a merlot, a Château de Millet cork screw and glasses. The prize though was a bottle of Armagnac from 1987 (the year of our high school graduation). As we were leaving, I asked in passing if she had a recommendation for a restaurant in Éauze that might be open on Mondays. She had a chart of restaurants open on any given day. She called the restaurant, La Vie en Rose, and made a reservation for us, mentioning we were Americans.

We made the short trip back to Éauze and found the restaurant near the center of town. We got there a couple minutes before noon. The waitress seemed confused when I mentioned "Laurent" had called for us. Recognizing my mistake, I corrected myself to "Laurence" which is a female name in France. She laughed and nodded with understanding; these were the Americans. The pretty outdoor terrasse across the street from the restaurant was decked out in pink (hence the name "rose," which is pink in French). It quickly filled up with locals. We felt lucky Laurence called for us as we saw many get turned away while lunch proceeded. Once again, we appeared to be a novelty with people at the closely spaced tables watching out the corner of their eyes. After we demonstrated manners and a little language, there was a palpable relaxation and an air of acceptance. The menu was exclusively in French and a little difficult to translate. Rather than pulling out our phones, we just went with it, picking out keywords to make our choices.

I started with a salad topped with duck breast and white beans. Courtney misunderstood a choice on the menu to be veal. After enjoying veal the first night in Gascony, she ordered "Poêlée de ris d'agneau" mistranslating lamb for veal. She loved the savory dish. It was only after the trip when I was adding descriptions to our pictures that I correctly translated the menu to reveal "pan fried lamb sweetbreads." Courtney now isn't so sure she likes lamb pancreas and thymus glands... but that day she did. My main course was duck confit which quickly became one of my go-to dishes. Courtney had cod with pork belly served with seasonal vegetables. For dessert, I had my first clafoutis in France, a dish I taught myself to make back in 2019 when we were first planning this trip. It is traditionally made with cherries but this one had prunes and Armagnac. When I made my first clafoutis, blackberries were in season, and it was so good, I've used blackberries ever since. My first clafoutis in France was excellent though I do have to say my own version stands up respectably. Courtney passed on dessert apparently filled up on sweetbreads. It was a great meal. After coffee, I used my bathroom hack to figure out I should pay at the counter. Our string of Gascon hospitality continued with the courteous staff.

We had some time before our next appointment and decided to wander the town's "centre ville" (downtown in French). Éauze has a rich history. The Elusates were a Celtic tribe who lived in Aquitaine during the Iron Age and Roman period. They were the last to surrender to Julius Caesar in his conquest of Gaul. Elusa (Éauze) was their capital on the banks of the Gélise River. During the Roman period, it became the capital of the Roman province of Novempopulania (Latin for "Land of the Nine Peoples") or today's Aquitaine. Rome's control of Gaul waned in the late third century. In an attempt to save the Empire, Diocletian recognized the provinces and tried to consolidate them. In the middle of the town square, we found a replica of a stone dating to the third century, discovered in 1660, which commemorated Verus' mission to Rome to resist this consolidation and demand they remain a separate province to preserve the area's sense of identity. Moving forward, the area was later invaded both by the Moors and the Vikings. As you can tell, I love history, and one regret I have was missing out on the Roman museum here. There are also Roman archeologic excavation sites in both Éauze and Montréal-du-Gers nearby which we skipped. I guess it gives me an excuse to return.

In the same square just outside the cathedral is the Fontaine Vital Dufour. The fountain celebrates the Cardinal and trained physician who gave us the first written evidence of Armagnac in 1310. In his medical treatise written in Latin, he extolls forty virtues of this "burning water." The original text is still closely guarded by the Vatican which infuriates modern day Gascons. The virtues include its ability to cure, among others, hepatitis, gout, cankers, fistulas and to heal wounds of the skin by application (which we proved without a doubt on Courtney's blisters in Paris). It goes on with my favorite part of the text:

> *"It enlivens the spirit, partaken in moderation, recalls the past to memory, renders men joyous, preserves youth and retards senility. And when retained in the mouth, it loosens the tongue and emboldens the wit."*

We had time to duck into Cathédrale Saint-Luperic. As far back as the third century, a bishop was based in Elusa. In the seventh century, the town had a bishop named Luperic who was later sanctified. After the Viking invasions, the bishopric was moved to Auch. The church, now technically no longer a cathedral, was built between 1463 and 1591. It was destroyed during the Religious Wars and rebuilt in the eighteenth century. It is of the Languedoc style with a single nave and six bays. The cathedral was an inviting space, full of light—a place to sit in quiet contemplation.

Our next stop was Delord Armagnac in tiny Lannepax. In my first book, I wrote extensively about falling in love with Armagnac over a bottle of "Delord 25 Years," and how I went on a difficult mission to find this product in America. This included emailing back and forth with Jerôme Delord, one of the two brothers who now run the business of this fourth-generation company which dates to 1893. After his help in 2014, I was hoping I might run into him. We were met in the reception area by a professional guide fluent in English. She started with an introduction to the company and its history. Part way through, I shared with her my story of petitioning the state of North Carolina for the right to buy Delord Armagnac. Later, finishing her spiel, she called out to Jerôme who happened to be walking by and introduced us. He stopped and shook our hands telling us he would be back for pictures during our tasting.

Our guide took us to see their stills in a warehouse a couple blocks away. They use gas fired stills and have both single and double distillation alembic stills. For their older, vintage Armagnacs, they use traditional single distillation. For their younger Armagnacs, they use a double distillation process which is allowed by AOC rules. This process allows a more consistent taste in their younger aged bottles. As we heard from several others in the business later in our trip, not everyone is so keen on this break from tradition. Our guide then took us to one of their larger warehouse cellars. In our path was an older gentleman, sweaty in work overalls. He backtracked across our path apologizing that he forgot his "chapeau." I quipped back he indeed needed it because of "beaucoup de soleil." When he passed by the second time, I had a flicker of recognition. I quickly asked the guide if he was the father, and she nodded yes; he was Jacques Delord, father to the two brothers Jerôme and Sylvain. I politely called after him to say hello. He came back and chatted amiably. I asked if he would take a picture with us. He said of course, but insisted "Pas ici." (Not here- in the industrial warehouse). Instead, he would meet us back at the main building.

We returned to the main building where we were taken back to see the bottling process. Three employees were managing the entire operation—one with a sauce pan of melted red wax, hand sealing and stamping each bottle with the Delord seal in powdered tin. They all waved and smiled while we watched them work. The guide told us a total of fourteen employees run the entire enterprise which has a world-wide distribution. She showed us the large metal containers where the Armagnac blends were mixed. We stepped over the clear hose delivering the current mix to the bottling operation.

We went through a side door into another cellar where the older vintages were kept. She explained the chalk signs on each barrel which noted the contents, the vintage, and the alcohol percentage (which changes with age and evaporation). Records are meticulously kept and are necessary for French tax purposes. Their blends are reduced to forty percent alcohol, but most of their vintage products are bottled at cask strength. She said with a smile that these were often sent to the Americans who have an obsession with cask strength liquors. She mentioned America had been their second biggest market but is currently taking on new importance. Their biggest market, Russia, is now gone with sanctions over the Ukraine War. Finally, she took us into the "Room of Paradise" where the extremely old Armagnacs were kept in glass bon-bonnes. After Armagnac has done its time in the barrel, it is transferred to these sealed glass containers where it does not age further. Some of the Armagnac in the room dated to 1900.

By this time, we were joined by Monsieur Jacques Delord who had taken the time to change his clothes, now dressed in a sporty V-necked sweater. He was quite jovial and mugged for the camera with us. He insisted our guide keep taking pictures until she took one he liked. He showed us his "desk" with a chuckle, a table filled with ancient bottles of every shape and size, graduated cylinders, tulip glasses and legal pads with handwritten, scribbled calculations. We thanked him for his time and expressed it was a great honor to meet him (and it was). We shook hands and said goodbye.

We returned to the reception room for a tasting and were offered a number of stellar vintages to try. While we were tasting, Jerôme hurried across the room to the door telling us not to leave before he came back. He had to pick up his daughter from school. I picked out a 1989 vintage bottle (the year of our marriage and the birth of our daughter), some Delord tulip glasses, and a bottle called Creation #12. For each "creation," the family picks out a blend of some of the best vintages to create a truly unique and special product. For each creation, they only produce a thousand bottles total. They were up to Creation #12 which is a blend of 1998, 1990 and 1973 vintages. I can't wait to open it. Jerôme, true to his word, returned to take pictures posing with me behind the tasting counter with all the bottles lined up. After making our bottle selections, the guide asked if we would mind waiting five or ten minutes while they got our purchase ready. I thought it was odd they didn't just pull them off the shelf for us. A few minutes later, we were called back to the bottling room and got to watch our bottles being hand sealed and stamped. Later in the trip, it was clear that not all producers agreed with Delord's particular business model. But, for me who first fell in love with Armagnac through Delord, this was truly a bucket list experience. That being said, the best was still to come.

We arrived back to Les Bruhasses by apéro hour which was a little more subdued tonight. It was only us and the woman on pilgrimage from Alexandria. Hélène and Jean were making a private dinner for their friends. Despite this Hélène made time to come out and pass me a handwritten note. She announced, "Your itinerary." She explained we had reservations and personal introductions to visit three Armagnac houses the next day. She was sending us further afield to the far western edge of Bas Armagnac, the so-called Grand-Bas-Armagnac region. She made us reservations at the closest domaine in the morning then suggested lunch in the town of La Bastide d'Armagnac before visiting the other two. For the last appointment, we were to ask for Josselin de Ravignan à Perquie. She told us we should not arrive before 4:30 or 5pm because Josselin would be working the vines in the afternoon. After she left us, we retired from the three-person cocktail party to have our picnic on the back terrasse.

It was a perfect night for a picnic. We opened a bottle of Château de Millet merlot and sliced our tomatoes and cucumbers to have with the bread from the market. After all the heavy food, a light dinner hit the spot. As Courtney lingered on the porch, I was drawn to the mesmerizing, slow sunset on the property. I got some terrific shots of the melting sun framed by spidery branched trees and the pigeonnerie. The vistas once again took me back took me back to my Nebraska roots. In the twilight, Courtney and I walked the grounds appreciating the beauty. After dusk, we returned to the back terrasse.

When we returned, Jean and his friend were there enjoying an after-dinner drink. We were embarrassed to have left our mess. They invited us to join them for an Armagnac. We declined since we still had wine left. We talked about sports, culture, and the astronomical cost of college in America. The ladies came out to join us, and the conversation continued. They asked us to stay, but we politely excused ourselves, not wanting to intrude on their time or force the conversation back to English. Heading back to our tower, we marveled at yet another spectacular day.

14

PIQUEPOULT

We got to breakfast earlier in preparation for a big day. Today's offering was banana bread flambéed in Armagnac plus all the other accompaniments. The conversation at the table was focused on the "Table d'Hôtes" planned for that evening. A day or two a week, Hélène makes a traditional, home cooked Gascon meal for her guests with paired wines and Armagnac, all-inclusive, for a remarkably reasonable price. According to the reviews, it is a fabulous experience. The dinner is traditionally served at 8:30pm. The issue at breakfast was the timing of the meal. The Idaho couple had complained they didn't eat that late in America. A little perturbed, Hélène told us she had reluctantly agreed to move it to 8pm. With a smile, I told her we would eat dinner whenever she wanted to cook it. She cautioned our last visit of the day had the potential to run long because Josselin de Ravignan was one of a kind.

Our morning visit was to Domaine de Paguy. Hélène let us know the current owner and operator of the business was out of town, but her father, Monsieur Darzacq, had agreed to give us a tour and tasting.

We should ask for him. We found the enchanting property at the end of a gravel road. Parking in the back, it appeared deserted. We walked around to the front past an inviting swimming pool to find an opulent, vine-covered home surrounded by vineyards all around. We still did not see any evidence of life or signage directing us toward a tasting. It felt a little like trespassing. I walked along the front of the home looking for a clue on how to proceed. I walked past an open-air window to find an elderly gentleman sitting at a table nodding off. I softly asked, "Monsiuer Darzacq?"

Startled, his first look was guarded with body language which read, "What are you doing on my property?" He had some trouble understanding my French and me, his accent, but I eventually explained we were here to taste his Armagnac. He brightened a bit. I then mentioned Hélène had sent us. At this, he produced a wide grin exclaiming that Hélène's father was a great friend of his (something he told us at least twice more during the visit). He came out and shook our hands then asked us to wait. He disappeared and returned with his granddaughter, whom he clearly adored, to translate. She was a charming young woman happy to help her grandfather.

Monsieur Darzacq led us to the tasting room which proudly displayed a multitude of trophies won by his domaine. Once he got behind the tasting bar, he was truly in his element. He gave us a lesson on tasting Armagnac—how to properly sample the "nose" before taking a sip. On the tip of your tongue, the initial explosion of flavor is called "The First Attack," after which you let it roll around your mouth to appreciate all the complexities. He was proud to explain that Domaine de Paguy specialized in single varietal (one grape) Armagnacs. He had us try three different single varietals. We liked the spicy Baco but decided we really loved the finesse of the unusual single varietal made from Folle Blache (the grape called "crazy white").

He excused himself for a minute and left us in the tasting room with his granddaughter. In the pause, she looked at me and asked if I'd like to try another and if so which one. Of course, I answered yes and whatever she suggested. She grabbed a forty-year-old bottle and poured me a sample just as Monsieur Darzacq came back through the door. The granddaughter looked up at him sheepishly as if she was in trouble and asked, "Is this okay?" He eyed the forty-year-old bottle and, after a pause, said yes. She let out an audible sigh of relief. It was heavenly but very expensive!

We ended up buying a bottle of his single varietal, Folle Blanche. He seemed pleased with our choice and was proud to show us the bottle was labeled "Piquepoult," an old name for Folle Blanche used in the region. The vintage year, 2002, was handwritten in yellow. We asked if he'd be willing to take a picture with us. He was clearly pleased with the request but joked it would cost us! I told him to "put it on the tab" which his granddaughter interpreted for him earning us a belly laugh. His granddaughter took the pictures. She was a real gem. She generously complimented us on our French, gave us restaurant recommendations for lunch, and even offered to call ahead for us; we thanked her but declined not wanting to impose further. Bidding us farewell, she invited us to walk around the other side of the grounds to view her father's exotic bird collection which was extensive and filled with exquisite specimens.

Labastide d'Armagnac was about a ten-minute drive. Founded in 1291 when Gascony still belonged to England, this is a town where time has stood still. Half-timbered buildings surround the quiet central square, Place Royale. The arched arcades are highlighted by flowering vines. Though one of Les Plus Beaux Villages de France, it feels undiscovered and untouched by the modern world. Arriving in the square at 12:00 sharp, we found the terrace of the restaurant Au Bastignac empty. Unsure if we could sit down, I made eye contact with the head waitress gesturing to a table near the door asking if it was okay. "Non," she said sternly. She explained the only table available on the terrace was at the far end. The tables did fill in later, but many remained empty. Despite having space, we saw several other parties turned away while the meal progressed. We never really understood this practice, which we witnessed at several other restaurants in the area. American restaurants would certainly never pass up a chance to fill all their tables.

We both chose the same options from the formula starting with jambon (delicious thinly sliced ham) wrapped around pieces of melon. We shared a small bottle of a local red which was very good. The melon was refreshing and was soon followed by a veal stew. (And this time it really was veal!) It was served family style in a large serving pan, enough to feed an army. It was full of ground veal and potatoes in a savory broth. It was very good though it was a hot soup on a hot day. We both had to decline dessert making a joke about how full we were. The stern welcome had softened into pleasant and smiling service. We observed this process several times. In southwest France, it seems outsiders are first viewed with some apprehension. You feel observed and at times tested. However, if proved to be polite and respectful, visitors are treated like family. In the end, it is quite possibly the friendliest region we have ever visited. I paid at the counter here, and we set off on our next adventure.

The next stop in Hélène's agenda was Château de Lacquy where we were to ask for Mme. Sandra Lemaréchal. I was excited for this visit because I knew of its reputation for producing some of the finest Armagnac—it is one of the so-called five "Cru Legendaires." The grounds are dominated by a spectacular castle featured in coffee table books. We met Sandra at an outbuilding which housed the tasting room and adjoining cellar (chai). Sandra was very professional and taught us some new things about Armagnac. They buy their barrels from two different, premier producers. Barrel making for Armagnac is truly an art and worthy of another whole chapter. She explained that the two barrels they buy are different in the terms of the width of their wood grain. This impacts both evaporation and the quality of tannins in the final product. For each vintage year, they age some of their Armagnac in each type of barrel producing two different tastes. Their chai, built in 1876, has a dirt floor and is vented to the outside. The variations in temperature and humidity add to the character and complexity of the Armagnac.

In addition to the Armagnac, Château de Lacquy has an incredible history. The aristocratic Boisseson family has crafted Armagnac here since 1711 making it the oldest family-owned producer. During the French Revolution, the Marquis de Boisseson fled to safety at the court of the Russian Czars. Due to his military experience, he rose to the rank of Major General of the Russian Empire. In the 1770s, he was responsible for sending troops to support America during the Revolutionary War. His son, Louis-Hercule, under the patronage of Czar Alexander I, served in the Imperial Guard. Louis-Hercule's son, Constantin, was the godson of the Czar's brother. The current owner of the estate, Count Gilles de Boisseson, is his direct descendent. To add to the history, during World War II, the widowed heir to the estate played a large role in the Resistance movement in France, aiding downed Allied pilots to escape to the safety of Spain. Our guide explained that one of the reasons Château de Lacquy doesn't have a lot of extremely old vintages is in part because the inventory was sold off during the war to support the Resistance.

The tasting room in the outbuilding was elegant. Everything we tasted was superb. I had almost settled on a bottle of twenty-one-year-old Armagnac. However, I ended up going with my gut to splurge on an exquisite bottle of their 1991 vintage (the year of our graduation from college). The reception area was at a distance from the castle. The view was mostly blocked by the grove of trees in between. There was a circular drive which passed closer to the château. I asked Sandra if it was okay to drive a little closer to get a view of the castle. She bristled a little at my question and discouraged us from doing so since it is still a family home. We did understand. In the end, though, the tour of Château de Lacquy, while luxurious and exuding quality, felt less personal than our other visits.

We had some time to kill before our next appointment which was not to occur before 4:30 pm. We had driven past Saint-Justin on our way to Château de Lacquy. From my research, I knew Saint-Justin to be an historic town. The town was small but did have a tidy, ancient square and a picturesque little church. It was sleepy and not much was open. After a quick tour, we drove a few blocks to a gift store we had seen on our way in. Courtney had gone into shopping withdrawal since leaving Paris. Unfortunately, the "gift" store was mostly food products and overall got a shrug from Courtney. Thus, we jumped in the car to head for Château de Ravignan.

The route to Ravignan took us deep into the countryside. There were no obvious signs, and Google Maps was confused. When it told us we had arrived at "votre destination," we pulled onto a narrow path leading to a cute little house that was definitely not a château. Sitting completely still in one of the windows was a little old lady dressed to the nines including a fancy French hat. She promptly came out to the car a little perplexed at our arrival. I asked in French where to find the castle. She was very gracious and nodded as if this had happened before, pointing us down a bend in the road. I tried to carefully back down the narrow path marked with reflectors since it cut directly through their lawn. As we pulled out, a man standing around the corner of a shed, presumably her husband, stared at our car suspiciously.

15

BUCKET LIST, PART TWO

You may have noticed that so far, each day of the trip has been covered by a single chapter. On many of those days, we had a number of fantastic experiences. I depart here because this one deserves its very own chapter—an experience so unique and extraordinary, so full of energy and fun, we will remember it forever. We followed the bend in the road which cut through a grove of trees. At the first break in the tree line, a jaw dropping view opened to our right that made me laugh out loud and exclaim, "Well, I think we found it!" Behind an ornate, wrought-iron gate stood a magnificent structure—a striking castle drawn for a storybook or maybe from a scene out of a Bond movie. As we parked and got out, our compact rental car looked ridiculously out of place.

For the second time that day, it wasn't clear where to go to announce our arrival. We took the only path we could, which ran between the iron fence and the adjacent twelfth-century church. We followed it to a couple outbuildings and what appeared to be the chai. A door was ajar in one of the buildings, behind which I could hear voices. I knocked, gently pushing the door a little further open while asking hesitantly, "Josselin de Ravignan à Perquie?" There stood a man in a simple shirt and shorts who had clearly been working. I introduced myself and Courtney in French. He answered in English, "Hello, nice to meet you. Hélène sent you?" He appeared a little embarrassed by his dress and indicated he was not ready for the tour. He invited us to stroll through his gardens while he changed into proper attire.

The gardens were artistically laid out in perfect harmony with the château. The grounds were filled with exotic botanical specimens and trees. Inside the gate, wandering through regal gardens at the foot of a sensational castle was surreal. About ten minutes later, Josselin was back, dressed in nice slacks and a polo shirt with the collar stylishly popped. He was on the phone talking for a few minutes (we later learned he was talking with Hélène). When he finished, he walked jauntily up the path to greet us like old friends. We immediately connected. His English was very good, and we tried to answer in French as much as possible. When he would get stuck in English, I would try to help by guessing the word. When I guessed right, he would answer, "Exactement!" with a jolly laugh. We chatted for about fifteen minutes covering a variety of topics: sports, what sports I had played, the popularity of rugby in the area, our son's rugby career, Josselin's limited experience with the United States, and his distributor in San Francisco, a man he clearly adored. He hadn't grown up playing rugby but was proud to tell us he was in the first wave of surfers when the craze hit Biaritz, adding that his first wetsuit was an American brand, O'Neal. He talked of his mother's Dutch/French heritage (a Dutch heritage he shares with Courtney) and of his father who learned his English while in Texas.

I have tried hard to think of words that would accurately capture his immediate, infectious energy and ebullient spirit, but am not sure I can convey the full picture. A 2018 quote from Craig Lane, the head bartender at a James Beard Award winning bar in San Francisco, sums up Josselin far better than I can:

"Though we have met and formed partnerships with great producers from top tier domaines throughout France, no one has been able to captivate our imagination more than Josselin de Ravignan. An avid surfer and a student of the French horn, Josselin cuts an impressive figure with impeccably coiffed hair framing cherubic features that can only be matched by his unparalleled sartorial elegance. It's as if he were a French duke from the 18th century inexplicably transported to our timeline, yet he managed to adapt himself effortlessly to modern technology like cell phones and cars, whilst still preserving his arcane regal demeanor."

The conversation turned to his home, and Josselin launched into a captivating tale of the history of both the castle and his family. I've tried to capture the story the best I can remember. Apologies for anything I misunderstood. A fortification was first built here in the Middle Ages owing to it defensive position protected by two large ravines (hence the eventual name Ravignan). In 1108, a fortified castle was built on its foundations. For a time, it sheltered a priory. Over the years, a variety of feudal lords occupied it. In 1565, it was burnt down by Calvinists during the Wars of Religion. On its ruins, a Louis XIII style manor house was built in 1663. This forms the current east wing of the castle.

This brings us to the de la Croix family. I do not remember all the details, but Josselin began his story describing a relative who won a large sum of money gambling. This eventually led to the family's involvement in minting coins in Bayonne. Jean-Baptiste-Dominique de la Croix was an ambitious young man who became involved in the maritime trade. With his business growing, he eventually became the director of the Bayonne mint and later the treasurer of the new Compagnie des Indies. He risked a significant portion of his assets on a boat to India and literally, his ship came in. At the same time, history records his involvement in financing expeditions of a famous Luzian corsair. In 1715, his wealth growing, he was able to purchase the post of Secretary to the King which conferred him nobility. When he died single, his fortune and title passed to his younger brother, a cavalry captain, also named Jean. In 1732, Jean de la Croix bought the lands of Perquie and the manor home at Ravignan, taking Ravignan as his last name. Vineyards were first planted that year and have now been cultivated by ten generations of his family.

That is an amazing story, but Josselin wasn't done. In the 1790s, two remarkable brothers were born into this family. The younger, Gustave de la Croix de Ravignan became a Jesuit preacher, professor and author who was named the chair of "the" Notre Dame in 1837. When he died a "saintly death" in 1858, it is reported thousands followed the remains of the "Apostle of Paris" to his grave. His older brother, Hippolyte, was no less accomplished. He was a calvary officer and later an aide-de-camp to one of Napoleon's generals. He was present at the Farewells of Fontainebleau where he received the Cross of the Legion of Honor from the hands of Napoleon himself. He returned to Ravignan and began to transform it into the structure it is today. He laid out plans to construct the west wing of the castle in perfect symmetry with the existing east wing. The elegant grounds and gardens were laid out by the renowned landscape artist, Eugène Buhler. The park was designed with studied vanishing lines and many unusual botanical specimens. For example, one of Josselin's relatives brought back Sequoia seeds from California. One of those seeds has now grown into a towering tree over one hundred years old.

Having spent about an hour on the lawn between the small talk and the history lesson, Josselin concluded with a question, "Now shall we go to cellar?" We walked around to the chai and entered its dark recesses. There was a man sitting quietly in the dim room applying labels to individual bottles. He addressed us in a twangy American accent, and I replied, "I can hear the Texas." He finished up his work and left the three of us in the tasting room. Josselin started by asking what we knew about Armagnac and if we needed a lesson. It was getting late, so I hinted we had already been to several domaines and had a pretty good understanding. As if he hadn't heard me, Josselin launched into a dissertation on Armagnac and his vision of the correct way to make it. I am so glad he did. A captivating raconteur, Josselin had unequivocal opinions on the artisanal crafting of this magical spirit. He gave us a history of Armagnac similar to others we had heard but never with such enthusiasm.

Several of the places we visited ferment and distill each grape variety separately then mix them later in specific ratios. Delord, for example, explained that most of their products are a defined mixture of more than 50 percent Ugni Blanc with smaller percentages of Columbard, Folle Blanche, and Baco respectively. In the Delord chai, the barrels were labeled with the variety of grape which was aging to later be mixed in the large metal vats before bottling. Josselin, on the other hand, explained they "let nature decide." They have plots of each type of grape. Annually, no matter what each plot yields, it all gets fermented and distilled together, no matter the ratio. This means every vintage year is completely different. He described one year when they had an early frost. At the time, only one variety had bloomed. Due to the frost, it yielded no grapes. Therefore, that year his Armagnac contained none of that variety.

He moved onto talking about the complexity of Armagnac in terms of the nose and taste. He observed, "People say they don't know Armagnac, and my answer is, I don't know Armagnac either." The beauty of Armagnac is in its variation. This is as opposed to the consistently same, and in my opinion, boring taste of Cognac. Cognac is the Hollywood blockbuster dumbed down for the masses. Armagnac is its Indie cousin, an art house masterpiece, lovingly crafted by its creator to be unique and exciting. Josselin noted there are more than 900 different producers of Armagnac, each making it with closely guarded methods passed down through generations of family. If each producer has on average thirty different blends and vintages, he pointed out this makes 27,000 different versions of the spirit. The joy is in the distinct taste of each. He went on to emphatically make the point that the tasting notes should not be defined by experts but instead, should be solely based on the individual as they immerse themselves in the experience.

Château de Ravignan is in the "Grand" Bas Armagnac region. It straddles the border between the Landes and the Gers departements. Closer to the coast, the domaine is very much more under the influence of the maritime climate. Its light, sandy soil produces delicate aromas. The wines are fermented naturally without enzymes, sulfites, or filtration. It takes five to seven liters of wine to produce one liter of Armagnac. As opposed to many others who, in search of profit, pump out higher volume, younger, and cheaper Armagnacs, Ravignan refuses to sell any Armagnac until it has been aged at least twelve years. He was proud to tell us that one of his vintages is especially famous (I think the 1985 but don't quote me on that). With its stock dwindling, they decided to stop selling it altogether, allowing the remaining precious elixir to continue to age and mature (and appreciate in cost). He boasted many of the most famous restaurants in Paris frequently call requesting to buy more, but he tells them nope, it isn't for sale at any price.

Josselin invited us to follow him deeper into his cellar. Stopping well down the long row of four-hundred-liter barrels, he looked at me and asked, "You didn't bring your glasses?" He was referring to the tulip glasses he had left on the tasting bar. I replied I didn't know we were supposed to. Courtney offered to go grab them and started jogging up the row, taking the first left instead of the second. I headed back down the row calling after Courtney, "You took the wrong left!" She was hopelessly lost in the depths of the chai. I looked at Josselin who started laughing hysterically. I returned to the tasting room to retrieve the glasses by which time Courtney had found her way back.

Now with our glasses in hand, Josselin announced ceremoniously,

"I want you to experience the difference in taste that aging in oak produces." He grabbed a long glass tube and removed the large plug, referred to as a bung, from a barrel of his 2017 vintage. "This is what a young Armagnac tastes like. Taste its fire, its spirit." He poured generous portions into our glasses before drinking himself, directly out of the tube. We both took a sip and let it roll around on our tongues. It had the powerful, aggressive explosion, "The First Attack," then was more fruit forward as younger Armagnacs go. He looked at Courtney now on her third tasting of the day and told her she didn't have to finish it all; he wouldn't be offended. She looked relieved and confessed she didn't need to finish it. He smiled and said, "Just pour it back in the barrel." Courtney looked startled at the thought. He encouraged her, "It's okay; its alcohol." I joked his 2017 vintage when bottled was going to be a sweet year now that Courtney was part of it. In seven years when Josselin is ready to sell it, we have vowed to buy a bottle, or a case, of 2017. Josselin looked at me and my glass. With a wink, I quickly replied, "Oh no, I am drinking everything you give me!" He grinned widely.

We proceeded down the row of barrels sampling progressively older vintages. While Armagnac ages, it eventually develops "rancio." The literal translation of rancio is rancid, but for Armagnac, rancio is an awesome thing. Rancio in old Armagnacs develops with oxidation of fatty acids into ketones (sorry my chemistry major is showing) which produces rich and unusual flavors. Rancio in Armagnac can be experienced as funky, musty flavors like leather, toasted nuts, tobacco, mushroom, butter, aged cheeses, over-ripe fruit, licorice, or even vanilla. Like Josselin pointed out there is no right answer—only what you, the individual, experiences. No matter how you define it, it is exceptional. We headed back to the tasting room to "begin" our tasting. I asked to use the bathroom at 6:15pm. When I returned, I apologized saying we didn't want to rush him, but we were supposed to be back at Les Bruhasses for dinner at 7:30pm, a thirty-minute drive (dinner was really at 8pm, but I thought Josselin was likely to run over). Josselin remarked, "Hmm, 7:30 seems very early."

After tasting directly from multiple barrels in the chai, we started our official "tasting." The conversation remained lively while we sampled some of his award-winning vintages. Courtney tasted one of them and said she picked up caramel notes. Josselin's face immediately took on a look of horror. I said, "Court, I think you have insulted him." Josselin recovered gracefully and said, "No, no, it's okay." We discussed how some producers use the shortcut of adding small amounts of an allowed caramel additive to artificially add taste and make the Armagnac appear older than it is. Josselin would never in his life consider this strategy, "Bien sur!" He told Courtney, he'd prefer she used tasting notes of "pastry" rather than caramel.

We ended up selecting a 1991 vintage, a gold medal winner. He approved of our choice. He reached under the counter and pulled out a jar of Raspberries Armagnac, his mother's recipe. We each tried one, and they were incredible. Courtney took my picture with Josselin who leaned in arm in arm. He abruptly asked for my cell number. He texted me his contact information and email address promising to put me in touch with his distributor in San Francisco. He told us the next time we visited he'd give us a tour of the inside of the castle and take us out to dinner. As we left, I told Josselin, "Ça a eté un grand plaisir!" which may have been the biggest understatements of the trip. When we made it to the rental car, it was after 7:30 and Google maps showed our arrival for the 8pm dinner at Les Bruhasses as 8:01pm.

16

LES BRUHASSES

Taking the prospect of being late to dinner as a challenge, I aimed to shave a few minutes off our arrival time. Always a fan of driving fast, it was nice to have an excuse to open it up on the country roads. Though worried about flying through one of the road-side radar traps, I thoroughly enjoyed running through the gears as we worked our way back to Les Bruhasses. In the end, I cut seven minutes off our half-hour drive, and at least at the time of this writing, I haven't received any speeding tickets by mail. We hurried out of the car; the guests were already seated. We met Hélène walking toward us telling us not to worry. She assumed we would be late. While we were waiting in his gardens, she had been on the phone with Josselin telling him we absolutely did not have time to tour the inside of the house. While we would have loved to tour the inside, I fear Hélène was right. We might not have made it back before midnight.

Hélène seated us next to a lovely older couple from Toulouse who were in the area for a wedding. They spoke almost no English, so it was a good opportunity to practice our language. Nobody else at the table made much effort to speak in French. We felt bad for this, and Courtney and I tried to compensate by engaging them while translating, the best we could, the conversation at the other end of the table. Next to us was a new couple from Australia who were very nice. Mercifully, Hélène had seated the three "pilgrims" at the other end of the table. Hélène and Jean were on roller skates rushing to serve each course and paired wine in seamless transition. The food was tremendous. One regret I have is that in trying to focus on thinking and speaking in French (which takes a lot of energy to sustain), I didn't allow myself to savor each dish the way I wish I would have.

Given my divided attention, it was hard to capture all the details, but I tried my best when I wrote later in the evening. The first course was a glass of gazpacho with a skewer across the rim with local figs and cheese along with a tasty piece of duck which had the consistency of jerky. Hélène explained gazpacho was one of her go-to's in the summer. The second course was also a gazpacho, but this one was made from zucchini. Spanning the rim of the bowl was a thin fried cylinder recalling the outside of an eggroll only this one was filled with local foie gras. The main dish was duck breast perfectly done, rare with a medley of savory local vegetables. Dessert was a layered torte doused with Armagnac. To finish off the meal, we were offered, of course, a Château de Millet Armagnac as a digestif.

The hikers excused themselves first, then the Aussies. We lingered over the Armagnac with the couple from Toulouse getting to know each other. He was a police officer retired from the Police Nationale. They were very proud of their son who was a successful satellite engineer. They were excited to tell us he was soon going to Kentucky to work on a project for his company. They described for us their beautiful city, "La Ville Rose" (the pink city) so named for the pink brick from which the "vieille ville" (old town) is constructed. In part due to their description and with Hélène's enthusiastic endorsement, we plan to spend a few days in Toulouse on our next trip. We ended the night showing each other pictures of our grandchildren.

As the night ended, we told Hélène and Jean what a wonderful time we had staying with them. I offered to be Jean's assistant groundskeeper, remarking I'd be happy to work for breakfast and Armagnac. We wanted the pleasant evening to go on forever, but eventually wished the Toulouse folks goodnight and headed back to our room. We were able to get mostly packed for the next leg of our journey. It was late by then. However, excited by the enthralling events of the past few days, I was too wound up to sleep. After Courtney went to bed, I poured another small Armagnac and stayed up writing down all I could remember.

The next morning, after packing the car, we were late to breakfast. Sitting down to our last meal, I realized I didn't want to leave. The Idaho people had Hélène cornered pushing for recommendations for a pedicure, a chiropractor, and a haircut. They didn't seem to listen or comprehend when Hélène explained that customs for pedicures were different in France and chiropractors were not commonly utilized. The woman from Alexandria was expounding on her walk of faith again. We were able to block out the noise and enjoy the pancakes, breads, and jam one last time. We thanked Hélène and Jean for their hospitality once again and asked if they'd take a picture with us. Jean agreed but said he was late to pick up his daughter, and she was going to be "pissed." I told him to blame it on the "ugly Americans." We called them back into the breakfast room to give them a thank you gift of chocolates from Paris. Hélène's response was, "Why?" She said she was just doing her job. I explained that after reading the reviews, we thought we might have a memorable experience, but the stay had exceeded our wildest dreams. We shared warm goodbyes, promising to return.

17

TIME TRAVELERS

We departed Les Bruhasses and headed toward the Dordogne and our new home base, Sarlat-la-Canéda, a three-hour drive. Before leaving the Gers completely, we stopped in Condom for an ATM. Other than the brief trip to the market, we had not really explored Condom. It just so happened that the ATM was near the cathedral. The church is an immense, buttressed structure, one of the last built in the Gothic style in southwest France. It was constructed from 1506 to 1531 and is dedicated to St. Peter. We decided to pop in for a quick visit and entered through the side door. It had a wide aisleless nave and remarkable stained-glass windows. Outside was the famous statue of the Four Musketeers—the fourth being, D'Artagnan, a Gascon and the main character in Dumas' classic tale. Courtney took pictures of me posing as the fifth musketeer. We had read there wasn't a lot to see in Condom, but by accident, we managed to experience the highlights during a fifteen-minute stop. Heading in the direction of the Dordogne, the landscape gradually changed from the undulating fields of Gascony to a hilly and more forested landscape.

Since we couldn't check-in at Sarlat until late afternoon, I had planned a stop at the bastide town of Monpazier for lunch and a quick visit. Bastide towns were planned communities in the Middle Ages. They were typically built in the thirteenth and fourteenth centuries by local lords to stimulate commerce. The fortified towns were built around a central square, most often arcaded. The square served as a market, around which a grid-like pattern of streets was built up. Wide roads led from the gates (where fees could be collected) to the central market. These main thoroughfares were built such that two horse-drawn carts could pass allowing traffic to move in and out the market place. You may remember Fourcès where we ate dinner one night in Gascony was a bastide town but with an unusual circular "square." Labastide d'Armagnac, as the name suggests, was another.

Monpazier was founded in 1284 by King Edward I of England. In the sixteenth century during the Wars of Religion, it played a prominent role in this violent era, falling into the hands of the Huguenots in 1574. Later, peasant revolts by rebels called "croquants" occurred in 1594 and 1637. One of the leaders of the croquants, a man named Buffarot, was caught and taken back to Monpazier. There in the public square where we now stood, he was tortured and broken on the wheel, a gruesome way to be executed. Arriving just before noon, there were very few people in the backdrop straight out of the Middle Ages. Most of the shops were closed. Unfortunately, after sitting in the car for an hour, my hip left me feeling miserable, and Courtney had caught my sinus infection from earlier on the trip. Instead of eating lunch, we instead found a pharmacy to buy pseudoephedrine and chose ice cream as a meal. If we had felt better, I am sure we would have enjoyed this well-preserved but sleepy town more than we did.

The drive to Sarlat-la-Canéda took us past a number of fortified, hilltop villages most with towering medieval castles. A major battle-ground during the Hundred Years' War, the Dordogne already felt different from Gascony. In Sarlat, we found our designated parking area which was up a very steep hill a couple blocks outside the old town. Steep hills and hip pain don't go together, so I drove back down and doubled parked while we quickly unloaded our luggage. Walking a block into town, we arrived at our Airbnb at precisely 3pm to find Hervé sitting outside waiting for us in the shade.

Hervé spoke virtually no English, so it was fortuitous our French had improved during the trip. He apologized for not speaking English explaining he never learned it well because he had been "a bad boy" in school. He was a nice young man and patiently explained how to work the appliances in the simplest French possible until we understood. Like Hélène, he suggested we trap the cool air in the morning, closing the shutters and curtains until evening. He gave us recommendations for boulangeries and grocery stores. Further, he went out of his way to warn us about a particular restaurant which, by his account, was a terrible tourist trap. He left us with welcome gifts—a bottle of Bergerac red and local, candied walnuts.

In addition to being unbelievably affordable (<$100/night), the place was fantastic. It was an unusual, three story detached house. Built in the 1300s, it had exposed brick and beams. There were little stone nooks built into the walls and a space which was once the firepit. It had originally been the home of a tradesman; the ground floor was his shop while the upper two floors were the living quarters. It had been meticulously restored leaving all the interesting historical features while updated with completely modern amenities. The ground floor was the main bedroom with an ensuite bathroom. The fully equipped kitchen and living room were found on the middle level. And, a second bed and bathroom constituted the top level. It was even better than the posted pictures; we couldn't believe our luck.

We were now exhausted and hungry. After a long day of travel, we didn't have the energy for a restaurant. We quickly unpacked and headed for the hypermarché, E. Leclerc. The giant store was initially overwhelming. Like all French grocery stores, the wine, cheese and yogurt sections were something to behold. We picked up yogurt, marvelous butter from Brittany, and two fruity jams to go with our daily baguettes. We got supplies for making a good salad, coffee, a few other cooking basics, and energy drinks to keep up the pace. I even found a pair of eight-euro flip-flops for our upcoming canoe trip. Unfortunately like a kid in a candy store, I fell into the grocery store wine trap. I ended up with a red, a rosé, and a bottle of the famous dessert wine, Monbazillac. After trying them, they weren't terrible (I actually really liked the sweet dessert wine, Courtney didn't). However, we vowed that in France forever more, we'd pass on grocery store wine and rely on the sommeliers at local wine shops to select our wine for us. Finishing up at E. Lerclerc, we managed the cashier's line proud to avoid any faux pas.

After a refreshing dinner, we decided to go out and explore the town. Sarlat-la-Canéda is an adorable, picturesque town which feels stuck in a time warp. The old town is virtually unchanged since medieval times. Though the exact date of its founding is unknown, Sarlat, which developed around a Benedictine abbey, has been in existence since the 800's. Due to its distance from the Dordogne River, about ten kilometers, it was the only abbey in the Périgord (another name for the region) to escape being plundered by Viking raids. In the Middle Ages, prosperous Sarlat was under the authority of the Pope. In 1181, King Philip Augustus of France pledged to protect the city. Then in 1279, the Black Death struck, killing half of the population. During the early phases of the Hundred Years' War, it was a French stronghold protected by the nearby defensive castles. In 1360, under the Treaty of Brétigny, it became English. It was eventually returned to France after England was finally defeated to end the war. Sarlat also played a key role in the Wars of Religion. Control of the city passed back and forth between Catholics and Protestants. In 1587, Protestants with an army of 6,000 men and four canons besieged the city defended by only 500 Catholic soldiers. Sarlat managed to hold out but not without damage. About a block from our place on Rue de Siège, one can still see Protestant cannon ball holes in the original ramparts.

We walked around town from amazing site to amazing site. Perfectly preserved, Sarlat feels like a movie set (as it has indeed been for multiple films shot here). After walking the circuit, we returned home for pain killers and some rest. Not wanting to waste the night though, we went back out after nightfall. In the dark, Sarlat transforms into something magical. Old-fashioned street lights give off a luminescent yellow glow creating dramatic highlights and shadows in the narrow maze-like alleys. In particular, our own street was stunning. Throughout the week when leaving through the front door, we would often inadvertently photo bomb tourists taking pictures of the street. Within a block or two of our rental property was the "Tour de Guet," a fifteenth-century watch tower with machicolations through which stones and burning objects could be dropped on attackers. Around the corner from us was the "Tour du Bourreau," the executioner's tower built in 1580 as part of the ramparts. So, I guess if you want to be technical, Sarlat is less of an idealized movie set and more of a brutal, Middle Age fortification.

I talked Courtney into stopping at a highly rated, off the beaten path, "dive bar." A connoisseur of dive bars, I had read reviews raving about the music and a friendly bartender. Courtney is more of a high-end cocktail bar kind of girl. Regarding us with a suspicious eye, the bartender wasn't friendly with us! This was clearly a local place not frequented by tourists. We struck up a conversation with a young man next to us at the bar. He was fascinated to talk with Americans. He had no idea where North Carolina was but clearly thought it exotic. He only spoke French, but we were able to understand each other okay. He talked about his life—growing up in Lourdes before moving to Sarlat to be near his brother. He was excited to tell us that he loved coming to this bar for the American rock and roll it played. Indeed, classic American rock was blasting in the background. I tried to engage the bartender telling him I liked his music, but he barely grunted in my direction. As it got later, a rougher crowd came in. Courtney became uncomfortable and hurried me out the door. Left to my own devices, I would have hung out all night. We later learned a nearby building was used for low-income housing.

We continued our walk around town and ended up wandering around the side of the immense cathedral to find an old graveyard next to the attached abbey. In the dark, eerie shadows were cast on ruins of rectangular stone gravesites without headstones; it was a little scary. Spookier still was the "Lanterne des Morts" on the hill above the graveyard. Many similar cylindrical towers were built across Europe in the 1100s, but this one is the tallest. No one knows for sure why these mysterious towers were built. Theories vary. Was it built to honor a visit by St. Bernard in 1146? Was it a true lantern for the dead or maybe just a funerary chapel? This one has an upper room in the second-floor cone which is completely inaccessible from the ground. Bizarre! Having finished our self-guided ghost tour of Sarlat, we headed home fairly early. With the time difference, we were able to video call our granddaughter, Cora, before getting a good night's sleep.

18

DEEP IN THE HEART OF TEXAS

I t is difficult to write anything linear about Sarlat-la-Canéda. Today's entry is a jumble of memories, the chaos of which is only rivaled by the labyrinth of blind alleys and secret passageways in this beguiling town. The plan today was to wander aimlessly seeing what we might discover. Before we set out to explore in the light of day, it was breakfast first. I walked a few blocks to one of my researched boulangeries to pick up a baguette and a pastry called Périgord Chocolat. Washed down with lots of coffee, we were ready to tackle the day.

We made our way down to the main shopping street, Rue de la République. I set off to locate the closest ATM for future reference. Courtney ducked into a gift shop owned by a lovely Madagascan woman. Her shop had lots of interesting jewelry, gifts, and spices from Madagascar. I wasn't there for their conversation in French, but it obviously made an impression. Later in the day, Courtney took me back to look at an interesting necklace made from light green polished stones. When we entered the store, the lady immediately recognized and greeted Courtney with a huge smile. She asked us to wait and walked out of the store. She went to the café next door and brought back her adult daughter pointing at Courtney explaining this was the American who spoke such good French. They both waited on Courtney who bought the necklace and a dress for Cora. The rest of the week, every time we walked down the street near the shop, they would recognize us and break their arms waving to us. When I got home, I found their store on Google Maps which was listed as "permanently closed." I notified Google that the store was most definitely open and left them their very first review full of superlatives for the shop and the hospitable people who worked there.

We spent the rest of the morning taking detours down interesting side streets and alley ways. However, for Courtney, all roads led back to the main shopping street! The shopkeepers were uniformly friendly especially when you observed the correct politeness. We stopped in a store called Blanc du Nil, which only carried sporty, white linen clothing. Courtney and I both saw things we liked on their sidewalk display and entered the store. Careful not to touch the merchandise, we told the shopkeeper what we were interested in. She helped us with sizes and recommendations. She pointed out to me, as I had heard before, that French sizes run small. I would definitively need the bigger size. She picked out items from the rack and gave us her full attention while we tried them on. In French, she kept up a running conversation interested in who we were and where we were from. We left the store happy with our purchases, and she wished us, "Bonne journée et bonnes vacances!"

We worked our way back toward our side of town and decided on takeout sandwiches for lunch. We chose a highly rated shop named simply, "Food & Co." The ratings weren't wrong. I ended up with a foie gras sandwich on baguette bread and Courtney a smoked salmon, all for twelve euros (less than we'd typically spend at Taco Bell). We took them home and washed them down with cold rosé from the fridge. Both sandwiches were top notch. After lunch, we rested in the shade of the house enjoying a siesta while letting our food digest. Refreshed, we headed back out for... more shopping.

Back on the shopping trail at a stylish shop called Un Autre Monde, Courtney fell in love with, I know this is hard to believe... a pair of shoes. Yet another shopkeeper was on point giving us her full attention. She commanded Courtney to try them on and then scratched her chin, studying the look before pronouncing them perfect. The statement was made as a matter of fact, not to be disagreed with. Courtney did agree they were perfect. Next, the shopkeeper pointed Courtney to a dress which would go well with the shoes. Courtney agreed again. She was directed behind the curtain to try it on. Similar to others in Sarlat, the shopkeeper was curious about us in a very genuine way. Courtney came out in the dress which was of the loose-fitting style currently in vogue. She said she wasn't sure and thought maybe it needed a belt. "Non!" came the stern answer. She illustrated her opinion by pointing to the pleats in back and tugging the dress tight. Her tone suggested that a belt with this kind of dress may well be against the law. Courtney asked, "C'est la mode?" "Oui," was the pronouncement. We walked out with a smile, a dress, and a pair of shoes. Like others, she waved to us from her shop the rest of the week whenever we walked by.

That afternoon, we explored the opposite side of old Sarlat starting in the ancient cemetery. It was still eerie but less so in broad daylight. When we reached the northeast corner of the old town, it started to thunder. We ducked into a shop here and there with hopes the weather would pass. However, light rain started shortly thereafter. We stopped at a cheap souvenir stand and bought Courtney a nine-euro rain hat. With the rain picking up, Courtney lost her enthusiasm for shopping. Darn! We made our way home to freshen up before our dinner reservations at 8:30pm. Back at our place, the sky opened up with a fierce thunderstorm. Despite its intensity, it passed quickly though the skies remained threatening.

Leaving plenty early, we drove roads just as narrow and crazy as in Gascony but much steeper. Looking for Restaurant La Terrace et Château La Bénéchie, we eventually turned left past a mailbox onto a dirt road. We approached a small château which appeared deserted. There was no signage or any clear evidence of a restaurant. It was 8:15. Not wanting to present ourselves too early, we sat in the car wondering if we were in the right spot. Closer to 8:30, we tentatively walked around the side of the château to the only place a "terrace" could be. We found it overlooking a valley. It had the feel of someone's personal back porch but did have five tables with tablecloths. A solitary man on a laptop was sitting with his back to us. Hesitantly, I asked in French, "Is this the right place?" He answered in American English, "Do you have a reservation?" We said, yes, we did for 8:30. He responded, "I had you down for 7:00." I was really embarrassed. It was one of the first reservations I had made in French months ago. I was sure the mistake was mine. He continued, "All my other tables called and cancelled because of the thunderstorm. You were the only table I didn't hear from." Not wanting to be an inconvenience, I started to backpaddle telling him we were sorry, and he certainly didn't have to feed us. He was very gracious and insisted we sit down; he'd be happy to cook for us adding, "Besides I was bored and just playing computer games."

The setting was incredible. The terrace overlooked a picturesque valley which after the storm was filled to the brim with a low fog. Delicate mosses growing out of cracks in the terrasse ledge held tiny droplets of water. The man returned with place settings and introduced himself as Arnie from Texas. He remarked that thunderstorms always scare the French away. We shared a laugh that a storm would never scare Midwesterners. He hadn't expected anyone to show, so he had just put the food away. The entire menu was handwritten on a chalkboard. There were only four items listed—three main dish choices: steak, duck, or trout and "dessert—four euros." Arnie assured us we would not go hungry because he served Texas not French-sized portions. I ordered steak cooked bleu, and Courtney went with trout.

Arnie returned a few minutes later with a wooden plank of food. Though no starters were mentioned on the menu, here they were—a loaf of bread, homemade aioli, and a round of Rocamadour goat cheese, hot and gooey. The pièce de resistance, though, was a large square mold of foie gras imbedded with local walnuts and sprinkled with candied bacon. It was by far the best expression of foie gras we ate on the trip. (And we ate a lot of it!) It was a melt in your mouth, while involuntarily moaning, kind of food. The accompanying bottle of Bergerac red was fabulous. While we were enjoying the first course, we asked Arnie how he ended up in the Dordogne.

Arnie proceeded to tell an extraordinary story. A young Hispanic man in West Texas, he started out teaching blind students in Spanish. He used to hang out at a bar where they knew him by name. The bar was attached to a fancy restaurant. One night after a few drinks, he heard the dishwasher had quit mid-shift. Arnie spoke up and said, "I can do that." He kept teaching during the day and washed dishes at night. He eventually worked his way up to making himself indispensable in the kitchen. The chef encouraged him to start culinary school which he managed to fit in on off-nights. His big break came when the head chef abruptly quit. The owner came to him and said, "Arnie, you know all the dishes. Why don't you take over?" He eventually finished culinary school on the side.

Sometime later, he entered a national barbeque contest with a friend from Oklahoma, by way of Norway, he had met in culinary school. They came in third. His friend told him he was opening a restaurant in Norway and asked Arnie to come work there. Arnie's answer, "Sure, but where is Norway?" Eventually working for a large restaurant consortium, he got to travel all over Europe working in five-star restaurants. Without an ounce of braggadocio but with more of a "I still can't believe it" tone, he mentioned in passing that he had cooked for the King and Queen of Norway, the King of Denmark, and numerous other famous people including Lenny Kravitz and Willie Nelson. We told him about our son who was at the beginning of a similar journey working his way up from the bottom with aspirations of becoming a chef. It was as if we were led to this place to see where Chad could potentially end of up on his quest.

Arnie met his wife in Norway, and when they decided they wanted a slower life, they moved to France and the countryside near Sarlat. They bought the small chateau turning it into a bed-and-breakfast. They worked hard on rehabbing the property and eventually opened it. Then, Arnie asked his wife, "What am I going to do now?" This led to the opening of his restaurant. He has five tables and cooks a limited, seasonal menu just for the joy of it. He is the cook, and his wife is the waitress. He told us it was the first day he had been open for the season. His wife wouldn't be back from Norway for two weeks, so it was just him (and the two of us) for the night.

He talked about learning to live in the countryside with the French. His neighbors were initially suspicious of an outsider, an American. However, when they saw how hard he was working his property, they quickly warmed. One neighbor helped with a lot of the work he couldn't do himself. Before his restaurant opened, another neighbor, an elderly woman, brought a full basket of truffles collected on her property (worth a veritable fortune) to get him started. He was proud to have assimilated. He uses all local products and smokes his meats with wood cut from his own property. Incredulous that the French don't age their beef, he buys his beef from the local boucherie and ages it himself.

On to the main dishes—Courtney's trout and pureed cauliflower was a work of art presented against a background of two different bright and savory sauces. We both had local potatoes quartered and perfectly fried in duck fat. Duck fat is our new fav—so tasty and, if done properly, not greasy at all. My ribeye steak was reverse seared then finished by smoking it on a giant Weber grill. The sauce was an absolute wonder. I asked Arnie how he made it. I won't give up his recipe, but suffice it to say, it is all day simmer involving garlic and a full bottle of local red wine finished off with a touch of sweetness. After the first bite, I couldn't have been happier.

The sky clearing, some of the fog had lifted. There were now brilliant streaks of pink and purple crowning the valley. The night was perfect. Dessert came next and like the rest of the meal, it did not disappoint. We were both served chopped Granny Smith apples and local walnuts bathed in caramel and butterscotch sauces served with vanilla ice cream. He offered us our choice of coffee or a local digestif made from prunes. Prunes from Dordogne are not for your grandmother's constitution but instead are sweet and delicious treats. The local digestif tasted a little like Armagnac and was very good.

When Arnie brought the bill, my jaw literally dropped. A magnificent three course dinner, cooked and served by a personal chef, along with a bottle of wine and a digestif all for a mere seventy-two euros! (Just shy of eighty dollars at the current exchange rate) I know you don't customarily tip big in France, but I handed Arnie two 50s and called it good. He protested and tried to refuse, but I insisted. It was the least we could do after arriving an hour-and-a-half late. We took selfies of the three of us and said our goodbyes. On our return, my online review of Arnie's place sang his praises and ended with, "And don't ever think of cancelling on account of a thunderstorm!"

19

PADDLING AWAY THE DAY

We were both excited for today. Almost every source you read tells you canoeing the Dordogne River is one of the highlights of any trip to this area. We had booked the earliest departure time available with Canoes Loisirs for the sixteen-kilometer paddle from Vitrac to Beynac. After the storms the day before, we were hopeful for better weather this morning. It was overcast as we drove to the launch point. The staff explained the details of the trip and the pickup process. Our directions were to pass under five bridges then veer to the left to find the docking area. They launched us, the first canoe for the day, and we were off. Our canoe was equipped with a waterproof container, though given our history of canoe disasters, we played it safe and left our phones and camera behind. We once capsized a canoe in a narrow, muddy channel of a mangrove swamp in Florida— just around the bend from a six-foot alligator! Given that trauma, I sat in the back and suggested I do all the paddling. In front, my wife, Queen Cleopatra, reclined in luxury.

The paddling was easy with the gentle current of the Dordogne

River pushing us along. A couple times a cross current turned us sideways, but there were no major mishaps. We saw a ton of waterfowl—mama ducks with lines of ducklings behind, a goose and its goslings, and even a pair of swans. There was a brief period of drizzle, but thanks to the nine-euro rain hat, it remained a good hair day. We didn't know to look for it, but the hilltop town of Domme, which we later visited, passed high over our left shoulders at the first twist in the river. The sky cleared, and it turned into a perfect day to be on the water.

At the next bend in the river, towering above us, was the spectacular La-Roque-Gageac (a "Plus Beaux Village of France"). The area is believed to have been inhabited since Prehistoric times. Built directly into the walls of a sheer cliff, it is an awesome site. At the top of several flights of rickety and impossibly steep wooden stairs are troglodyte caves. High in the cliff face, these caves were fortified safe havens for locals going back hundreds of years to the ninth century. A castle was visible at the far end of town. A deserted pebble beach jutted out from the undeveloped left bank. Though still a little early, we decided it was a great place for a picnic lunch. At home, we had debated whether to pack the Carré Blanc picnic blanket we bought on our first trip to France. Now we were happy we did. With a panoramic view of La-Roque-Gageac, we assembled our gourmet lunch on the blanket—a round of the famous Rocamadour goat cheese, a truffle cheese, and a funky, hard cheese purchased at the market in Sarlat. To the cheese, we added spicy sausage, peaches, and melon. Washed down with a Bergerac red served in paper cups, the leisurely lunch in a perfect setting is one of those events never forgotten.

Back on the water, we several times had to steer out of the path of gabarres. These are the traditional flat bottom boats which have been used for transporting goods on the Dordogne River since the Middle Ages. No longer used for commerce, they now carry boatloads of tourists up and down the river. While the boat rides looked pleasant enough, we agreed we much preferred our canoe ride for two. The slow but steady pace of the winding river was incredibly relaxing. At the next bend, at the top of a steep hill, was the imposing Château de Castelnaud-la Chapelle. The Dordogne River during the Hundred Years' War marked the border between French and English territories. For most of this extended conflict, this left bank fortification was an English stronghold, commanding views down both directions of the river. Viewing medieval castles from the water below cannot be beat.

At the bend in the river at Castelnaud, yet another castle, Château de Beynac, came into view. This right bank castle was for much of the war a French possession. I use the expression "for much of the war" because the two castles changed hands several times over the course of the Hundred Years' War. From their respective watchtowers, the French and English never took their eyes off each other. Like Castelnaud, the stark and ominous Château de Beynac rises strikingly out of the top of a sheer cliff. The way Beynac is situated, we had dazzling views both coming and going. Shortly thereafter, we passed under the fifth bridge steering toward the left bank drop-off point. Leaving the canoe on site, the shuttle back to our car was there within minutes. Reflecting on the trip now, this morning frequently comes up as one of the most memorable experiences.

Leaving the canoe home base at Vitrac, we drove across the river and turned right (upstream) to see yet another castle. This one, Château de Monfort, is privately owned, so it was a brief detour. We drove past it to get some good long shots then traveled fifteen minutes home to freshen up and plan the rest of the afternoon. I had loosely planned this stretch of the trip with many possible sights to be toured as they best fit the day. We debated and decided on a visit to Castelnaud before it closed in the late afternoon. Online, combination tickets with the Les Jardins Suspendus (the suspended gardens) de Marqueyssac were just a few euros more so we bought these for a visit to the gardens later in the week.

Château de Castelnaud-la Chapelle was first built in the twelfth century. Its owner, Bernard de Casnac sided with the Cathars in the

Albigensian Crusade. The Cathars were an anti-materialistic and dualist Christian sect eventually declared heretical by Pope Innocent III. The crusade effectively eliminated the Cathar religion and is now considered, by some historians, a genocide. During this "crusade" in 1214, Simon de Montford took the castle from Casnac. A year later, Casnac took it back and hanged the entire occupying garrison. Casnac lost his castle again, this time to the Archbishop of Bordeaux who ordered the castle burned to the ground. The castle was rebuilt later in the thirteenth century during the Hundred Years' War as part of English ruled Aquitaine. It changed hands several times during the war, once after a protracted siege by the French. By the time of the French Revolution, it had been abandoned and left in ruin.

In the 1960s, the current owners bought the castle and have painstakingly restored it. It is now an impressive museum. It was a steep climb from the parking lot made difficult by my hip but was worth the effort. It had exhibits of medieval weapons, armor and even a throne. Views from the top of the castle were breathtaking and just down the river, rival Château de Beynac was easily in view. There were well done, short educational videos and reconstructed siege weapons (that actually work). We both enjoyed it, me especially. With knights in shining armor and tales of epic battles, it is a place that is made for the little boy (and little girl) in all of us. Not so epic was when, gawking at the exhibits ahead, I missed a stair and fell twisting my ankle. For a moment, I thought I was badly injured but luckily was able to walk it off. We both agreed touring Castelnaud made us want to visit the museum of the Middle Ages, the Cluny, on our next trip to Paris.

On our way back to Sarlat, we stopped at a branch of Julien de Savignac's wine shops. I learned about this remarkable shop while reading the *Bruno's* series of novels by Martin Walker. The main character, Bruno, a likeable, small-town police chief solves fictional crimes though the settings and sights described in the book are real Dordogne locations. Fast and easy summer reads, they provide a nice window on local sites, customs, and culture. It was close to closing time. We took a chance illegally parking, given we planned a quick stop. We walked in to greet the sommelier/shopkeeper and asked for his suggestions for local wines we wanted to try. He was helpful and decisive, walking directly to each section to pick out bottles for us (a rosé, a Cahors and a Madiran). All three ended up being both excellent and inexpensive. So, "Bruno's" first recommendation was a great one—with more to come!

Tired from a long day, we decided to eat in. I walked down to our sandwich shop for takeout. Unfortunately, it was closed. Going next door to a small grocer, I left with tomatoes, cucumbers, nectarines, and local walnuts all for less than five euros. We enjoyed the light and healthy meal with some wine from Julien's. We had planned to go back out on the town. However, with rain again on the radar, we chose to stay in so we could be up early for the big Saturday market in Sarlat. It was a great choice because before long, a hellacious lightning storm broke out. With our windows open to the storm, the thunder echoed off the stone and lightning flashed in our dim fourteenth century home. It wasn't hard to imagine life in the Middle Ages.

20

EATING AT GRANDMA'S HOUSE

S aturday is market day in Sarlat. Getting started later than we wanted, the town was already packed. Vendor stalls filled every nook and cranny of the old town and beyond. The scene was a little overwhelming. The meat and produce stands were in the center of town while stalls selling everything else you could imagine lined the main shopping street. Other than Courtney's desire to look for salt and pepper shakers and her continued search for a straw bag, we didn't have much of a plan. We meandered through the fresh food section trying to remember where to find the best offerings in the maze of alleys. There were several pop-up stands selling from giant skillets—paella, sausages, Mediterranean dishes and more. It all smelled terrific. Courtney was interested in the paella but wanted to keep shopping until lunch time.

We worked our way to the flea market area and found ourselves disappointed. Most of the offerings were inexpensive, low-quality bric-à-brac. Here and there, you could find some better-quality goods, but it was slim pickings overall. Courtney did make a couple clothing purchases and bought a pair of "hugging" salt and pepper shakers from a jolly salesman. He wanted us to know it was a French (and not an English) set, explaining the English prefer their pepper to flow more freely than their salt. With a wink, I shot back at him, "Well the English do a lot of things backwards!" He laughed heartily at my joke. The centuries old rivalry was clearly alive and well. On a side note, on our return to America, I promptly dropped and broke Courtney's saltshaker. I was able to redeem myself, though, by finding a much cooler pair, antiques from France, on eBay.

By the time we got to the end of the market, it was hot and the entire street was shoulder to shoulder. Hungry and wanting to escape, we headed back in the direction of paella. At the paella stand, the huge skillet was now nearly empty and what was left looked like it had sat out too long. We decided to head back to the fresh food section and cook at home. We bought a savory loaf of bread and produce for a salad. Seafood sounded good, so we headed to the best fish stand. We picked out good looking filets though couldn't translate the name of the fish. We asked in French for the translation in English and got the infamous French shrug. She didn't know either. As she was ringing us up, we spied a pile of sea asparagus and had her add some to our tab. Everything we bought was amazingly affordable.

Home in the shade for our two-hour French lunch, Courtney made the salad while I worked on the fish. I chopped a couple fresh shallots and sauteed them in the butter from Brittany until caramelized. I added the filets with salt and pepper and seared them lightly on each side. On a whim, I deglazed the pan with the sweet white wine and poured the mixture over the filets, garnishing them with sea asparagus. We were quite happy with our tasty lunch, at least until later... Our new vacation rule is to never cook fish in an ancient rental place unless you want to smell it for the rest of your stay! Refreshed after lunch, we decided to use our tickets for the gardens.

Starting off with low expectations, we thought Les Jardins Suspendus de Marqueyssac would be a quick visit. We were wrong. The gardens are atop a rocky outcropping 425 feet above the Dordogne River with panoramic views of several nearby castles and scenic towns. The fifty-five-acre property has been owned by the same family since 1692. Toward the end of the nineteenth century, the gardens were improved with the addition of tens of thousands of boxwoods which are perfectly manicured in artistic, whimsical patterns. Live peacocks roam the grounds. There are miles of pathways traversing both perfectly coifed gardens and large stretches left wild. Along the way, we saw playgrounds for little ones and a climbing school with school-aged children suspended on ropes far down the cliffs. From every ledge and corner of the garden, there was a bird's-eye view of a spectacular site—the castles of Beynac, Castelnaud, and Monfort and the town of La-Roque-Gageac to name a few. We could trace the course of our canoe trip and see the pebble beach where we ate lunch. Walking through the forest, impressionist paintings behind glass displays were sprinkled throughout. There was even a unique stegosaurus sculpture where they have let nature take over with green growth covering its every surface. Completing the circuit, we were both overheating, and I was limping badly. Thankfully, we ran into the tea garden which was attached to a small restored château. Courtney had a Coca-Cola served with ice, a rarity. I had a local amber microbrew which was surprisingly quite good. Our add-on, dual tickets were definitely a good value!

Still mid-afternoon, we decided to visit La-Roque-Gageac only seven minutes away. This is the previously described town built into the side of a cliff. After finding a spot in a paid parking area crawling with tourists, we walked up a few inclines and a flight of stairs to the first upper level. Here, there was a fourteenth century church and unusual tropical vegetation. Owing to the sheer cliff's southward facing direction, the small town supports a microclimate where banana trees, bamboo, cactus and palm trees all thrive. I was looking for the stairs to the twelfth- century troglodyte fort, excited by both the history and the views from high on the cliff. I hadn't mentioned to Courtney that a landslide in 1957 had destroyed six houses and killed three people, or that in 2010, the village had to be evacuated after which part of the fort collapsed. The area was closed for many years to be stabilized and only opened again in 2020. We found the entrance to the steep wooden stairway. It cost seven euros to go up. At this point in the afternoon with the cliff face in full sun, it was deadly hot and humid. We made one of our best decisions of the trip and chose not to climb the 140+ stairs. Besides, Courtney would have killed me if she had climbed them only to find out later the potential for disaster.

Getting back to the air conditioning of our car, I mapped us home. The fastest route available was the same road we had driven down. Always interested in seeing new terrain, I chose the longer, scenic route. Well, maybe it was scenic, but the backroads were some of the narrowest of the trip. Without much warning, I was on a "two-way" road boxed in on either side by medieval stone buildings. There was barely enough space to fit our compact car as it was. Ahead a half mile of so, I could see the road open up. Fearing I'd have to back my way out of this mess if another car approached from the other direction, I stepped on it hoping to make it safely to the widening. It seemed like a great plan until one of the ancient buildings on the passenger side jutted out unexpectedly. With my eyes forward on the road ahead, I didn't see it coming. After the "SMACK," the spring-loaded side mirror had snapped back flush with the car. I made it to the clearing before stopping to get out (cursing a blue streak) to assess the damage. Luckily, the side mirror snapped right back into place. Inspecting the upper part of the mirror, I could only detect a tiny speck of missing paint which could easily be mistaken for one of the many dead bugs already stuck to the white car. Relieved it wasn't worse, we headed home to change out of our sweaty clothes before dinner.

We had 8:30 reservations at a restaurant in the countryside, "La Borie Blanche," ten minutes outside of Domme. It was one of my TripAdvisor finds with glowing, mostly French reviews. We were ready well ahead of time and decided to first visit Domme which was on our "to-see" list. Visiting in the evening was a great idea because the town had emptied of most of the day- tripping tourists. This left it with a deserted, ancient feel. Domme, yet another of Les Plus Beaux Villages de France, has an interesting history. It was founded by King Philip III ("The Bold") of France in 1281 during the Albigensian Crusade in part to check English expansion in the area. It is a trapezoidal bastide town owing to its geography. It was fortified on three sides except the cliff face which was felt to be impregnable. Domme sits atop a large hill, five hundred feet above the Dordogne River. During the Hundred Years' War, the town was captured by the English in 1348. It changed hands several times during the conflict before the French won it back for good in 1437. It also played a role in the Wars of Religion. Domme was a Catholic stronghold. In 1588, Geoffroi de Vivans, a Protestant captain from the Castelnaud garrison, scaled the sheer cliff face in the dark to open the gates to his troops who captured the town.

Domme was one of our favorite towns of the entire trip. It is a perfectly preserved, cute little village. It had numerous shops and restaurants though most were closed at the hour of our visit. The panoramic views from the cliff face, along which there is a walking path, were absolutely gorgeous. A French couple was very gracious in taking our picture at one of the overlooks, and we returned the favor for them. The sky was stunning with the sun poking through dramatically drawn rain clouds in the distance. Like many places in southwest France, touring the town felt like walking back in time. The centuries-old buildings were covered with attractive flowers everywhere. If we return to the Dordogne in the future, we would definitely consider staying here.

In Domme, much of the ramparts remain intact along with three of the original gates to the city. The coolest of the three is the Porte des Tours, an arched gateway between two large, round turrets. In the towers, seventy Templar knights condemned to death were held here in prison cells from 1307 to 1318. They left behind copious amounts of graffiti with obscure Templar references and symbolism. You can tour these cells, but the tower is only open during the day. Nevertheless, standing outside the town appreciating the austere immensity of the towers, I felt like a character in a Dan Brown novel.

It was another country roads adventure to find La Borie Blanche. Driving through forested land and wide-open fields without any sign of civilization, Courtney kept asking me if I was sure I had correctly mapped our route to the auberge. "Auberge" roughly translates to "inn" but often refers to a farm-to-table restaurant. "Farm-to-table" is currently a hipster term in American restaurant culture. Farm-to-table at a French auberge means exactly that. It is typically a restaurant on a working family farm where nearly everything you eat is produced on site. This time, there was actually a small sign across the road advertising the restaurant so at least we knew we were in the right spot. There was a gravel parking lot around the corner where several other cars were parked. Arriving at 8:15, we decided to go ahead and present ourselves early after our screw up with Arnie. We walked around to the farmyard which was surrounded on three sides with buildings. It wasn't clear which was the restaurant. Suddenly, the top of a half door swung open and a young woman leaned out on the lower half. She looked us up and down with an appraising eye but didn't speak. From the middle of the yard, I said in halting French, "We have a reservation?" She hesitated a moment considering the statement, then pointed at the next door down, again without speaking.

Before we could reach for the handle, the next door was opened for us, and we were faced with a small, older woman in a surgical mask holding a bottle of hand sanitizer. I repeated we had a reservation, and with little affect, all she said was "Oui," pointing to the only empty table inside the door. The other tables were all in animated conversation, but with our arrival, it became very quiet. Nearly everyone paused to check us out, some with subtle glances and others straight staring. It was immediately clear that we were "not from here…" There was a general air of wariness. The older woman returned with a pitcher of water, two water glasses and menus which she tossed on the table. She said something in staccato French I couldn't understand. It was clear she spoke little to no English. She abruptly walked away leaving us to our menus.

We surveyed the room which had gone back to lively conversation. It had walls of rustic stone around a fireplace and mantle. There were six tables in all, basically butcher-block wooden picnic tables with benches on either side. With chatter back and forth between tables, these were certainly locals who knew each other. We were clearly the only foreigners in the crowd. The menu had three separate formulas from which to choose: a basic four-course meal for nineteen euros, an upscale four-course meal for twenty-five euros and a grand five-course feast for thirty-four euros. On the drink menu was Vin de Noix. I had been looking for Vin de Noix since arriving in the Dordogne. Vin de Noix was another morsel I had gleaned from the *Bruno* novels. In the novels, Vin de Noix (literally walnut wine) is described in detail as an apéritif made by nearly every farmer in the area from liquor, wine, and green walnuts. I really wanted to try it. On the apéritif menu was also Vin de Pêche which Courtney decided to order.

When the older woman returned, there was a mild look of surprise behind her mask when I started out in passable French with, "Nous voudrions commencer avec des aperitifs, s'il vous plaît." Her surprise increased when I ordered Vin de Noix, and Courtney in turn asked for Vin de Pêche. She returned with a much softer gaze and proudly placed two small shot glasses in front of us. The room once again became quiet, people sneaking glances at our table. There was now a low murmur. I actually saw a man at another table nudge another and nod toward us. The conversation picked up again, the air of suspiciousness now evaporated. We had passed some sort of test. Bruno to the rescue again! I really loved the Vin de Noix which is complex and hard to describe—a rich almost syrupy dark liquid with layers of flavor favoring port. Courtney's Vin de Pêche was equally good. They were served with a bowl of local walnuts. When the woman returned to take our order, I explained it was my first-time tasting Vin de Noix, and it was "formidable." She smiled at this and said definitively in French, "I made that." Courtney likewise complimented the Vin de Pêche to which she responded, "I made that too." Courtney ordered the middle formula. I thought, "What the heck?" and ordered the grand feast. The woman paused, considering me, and answered, "Oh, you must be hungry!" We ordered a bottle of Bergerac red. When it arrived, it took us a minute to figure out both the wine and the water were to be drunk from the same glass.

The first course arrived in a large pot, family style. It was a hearty white bean soup with chunks of French bread. We ate it all and again complimented the woman whom we later learned was the mother of the young woman who had "greeted" us. They were the wait staff, and her husband was the cook. She was pleased we liked the soup but maybe more so that we had cleaned up our plates. For the next course, Courtney was served homemade beef pate. I was presented with a large round of duck foie gras but told I was not to eat it until she returned. She came back with small dishes of Fleur de Sel and fig preserves "de la maison." I was instructed to smear the preserves on a chunk of bread followed by a slice of the foie gras then lightly sprinkle with the salt. It was heavenly. Court's was good too.

After some time to digest, she arrived with our steaks. Though thinly cut, they filled the entire plate, mine "bleu" and Courtney's "moyen" (medium). She quickly returned with the pan in which the steaks had been cooked and asked if we would like the juice poured over. "Bien sur!" was our answer. The beef tasted Nebraska fresh and was very flavorful. We were served a side dish, a family style bowl of potato quarters baked first and then, of course, fried in duck fat (and again not greasy at all). During the main course, the husband came out in his apron to "talk" with people at one of the tables—obviously friends of his. As he did, it seemed clear he'd come out to take a peek at the Americans in his restaurant. Finishing up with the steaks, a thunderous storm rolled through. The other tables were paid up and leaving. Everyone had to make a run for it. The woman kept asking us where we were staying, concerned about our twenty-minute trip back to Sarlat on a dark and stormy night.

Next came dessert. The woman started with Courtney, explaining to her she had her choice of four different desserts-"gateau avec fruits de mon jardin" (cake with fruits from my garden), walnut cake, fromage de la maison (cheese made on site), and a chocolate dessert. Courtney chose the cake with fresh fruit. I started to order a different option so we could try two of them. She stopped me cold with a "Non!" and walked away. A little confused, I wondered if I had done something wrong. She brought Courtney's cake with fresh raspberries on top that were also baked into the crust then left again. I sat there not knowing what to do. She came back out this time with a large platter. Her eyes smiled behind her mask as she presented me with the plate. In French she said, "For you, you get all the desserts!" I had all the choices including one not mentioned- crème fraîche with candied walnuts atop a custard. All homemade and from scratch, they were fantastic.

While we finished dessert, she was really pushing coffee, again maybe worried about our trip home? We relented and agreed to a coffee so long as it was decaf. We were the last table left, and she was clearing the other tables. I tried to call her over. With a handful of dishes, she said sternly, "Non," and returned to the kitchen. Arms unencumbered, she returned to see what I wanted. The best I could, I explained we were from North Carolina (having to explain its approximate location) but that we had grown up in Nebraska in the center of America. Nebraska was cattle country, I continued, and my grandfather was a cattle rancher (translating rancher proved difficult but she eventually understood). I told her my grandmother was a farmer's wife and an incredible cook always preparing everything fresh off the land. Then I added, "Cela me rapalle la maison de mes grands-parents." (This reminds me of my grandparents' house) She smiled again but then added, "Everyone says that!"

She wanted to know how we had found her restaurant so far out in the country. I explained I read French better than I speak it and had read many stellar reviews online. We had trouble translating "reviews" but went back and forth until she understood "comments." I explained to her we always look for authentic experiences, and this meal was perfect. I told her I planned to write an excellent, online "comment" once I got back to America. Continuing the conversation, she told us she actually has some American friends from "Uu-tah." When the couple first moved to France, they had come to her restaurant. When finished, the husband tried to pay by credit card (they only take cash). The wife stayed and talked with the family while the husband drove all the way to Domme to find an ATM. Ever since, they have been good friends. She concluded in French, "Now that's a good story!"

She asked if we had children and wanted to know their ages and what kind of work they did. We talked about all three of our children and their lives. She was interested in Chad quitting his teaching job to pursue a career as a chef. She agreed teaching was a hard job and that one should follow their passion. Courtney chimed in to say in French that the true joy in our life was our granddaughter, "une petite fille qui a dix-huit mois." We showed her pictures which she loved. Concluding the conversation, the woman gave me her card. It listed the address of the restaurant, her name, Madame Borde, and their email address. I thought she was asking me to send her an email or write a review. "Pas un e-mail," she insisted. It took a while to understand that she wanted us to send her a postcard from North Carolina. We thought what a delightful idea—sending postcards from home to anyone who went out of their way to make our trip special. Back home, I wrote her a glowing review and sent her and several others postcards from North Carolina thanking them for their kindness. As I write this, three months after our return, my review and eight posted pictures have a combined 22,000 views. After a fond goodbye, we walked to our car. The storm had passed but we could still see it on the horizon, highlighted in the waning purples and oranges of a glorious sunset. During our slow and careful drive home, we marveled at how amazing experiences just kept happening on this unbelievable trip.

21

THE 16,000-YEAR-OLD WOMAN

After La Borie Blanche, Courtney was up early, but I was knocked out. It was slow going when I did wake up. I guess you have to watch out for Vin de Noix. Our morning plan was to drive a half-hour west to Saint-Cyprien for its famous weekly market. The town is named after a religious hermit, Cyprien, who came to the region and settled in a nearby cave around 620. Due to many reported miracles at this cave, a monastic community developed in what was to become the town. In 848, barbarian invasions forced the monks to seek safety behind the monastery walls. Saint-Cyprien shares a similar history with most other towns in the area. Given its position on the border of French and English lands, it suffered during the Hundred Years' War. Then in 1568 during the Wars of Religion, the village and abbey were burnt down by Protestants forces. They were later partially rebuilt. During the French Revolution, the church was transformed into "The Temple of Reason" dedicated to "the supreme being." The current day village hosts an authentic weekly market and has a well-preserved historic section.

We arrived at the market an hour later than planned, but the market was still just getting started. We snagged a good parking place and slowly made our way down the main street. Every few feet, the street had wire arches overtop it from which thousands of colorful purple, yellow, and red plastic streamers hung festively. Like most places in southwest France, we saw few tourists and heard nothing but French. The market was a foodie paradise with a wide variety of meats and produce. On our first pass, one notable stall had six large rotisserie hams rotating above a grill on which various other chunks of meat sizzled. It smelled amazing. At the very end of the street, Courtney found her straw purse. We bought it from a jovial Madagascan man. With charming interactions both here and in Sarlat, we both agreed that maybe we should consider adding Madagascar, the isolated island formerly part of the French colonial empire, to our bucket list. Courtney also bought a scarf from a nice French woman with a little bit of English.

On our way back down the street, we stopped at a cute cafe under the streamers for some caffeine. Court had a café crème, and I went for a double. The terrace tables were tightly packed, and two French couples practically had to climb over us to the get to the adjacent table. On hearing our English, they seemed intrigued but a little standoffish. But when Courtney politely moved her chair to give them plenty of room, they warmed considerably. Trying to shake off my grogginess, I made a joke about caffeine while ordering a second double café. I used the bathroom trick to pay and off we went.

After surveying the produce, we purchased ancienne tomatoes, cucumbers, purple garlic, and three unusual types of mushrooms. Walking back past the rotisserie stand, the giant hams were almost completely gone with just a few small slices left to sell. Courtney got a spring roll from a Vietnamese stand that smelled wonderful. I was laser-focused on a food truck, complete with an actual zinc bar, selling oysters. I had read the French white wine, Viognier, paired well with oysters. I had never tasted it and wasn't sure how to pronounce it. I ordered a half dozen oysters from the coast of Normandy and tried my best to order two glasses of Viognier. As I attempted to order the wine, I raised my tone at the end of the word making it into a question. The woman at the bar smiled and pleasantly corrected me ("vee-oh-Nyay"). I tried again and was close enough to get a nod. The oysters were salty, a little like east coast American oysters but with a very smooth finish. They were the perfect little snack before lunch. The wine was good too.

I was looking forward to lunch. I had made reservations for noon on The Fork app. It was the easiest of all the reservations I made. From the pictures, it was a picturesque countryside terrace where a talented chef cooked first-rate food. The reviews praised the quality and the view. Before leaving for the restaurant, we had time to walk through the medieval part of Saint-Cyprien which was quaint. Back to the car for a ten-minute drive, we cruised country roads once again. We actually ran into a wedding party filling the road in front of us. They appeared to be walking from the ceremony to the reception. The crowd was jubilant. Those in the back motioned to see if we wanted to pass by, but we shook our heads no, not wanting to disrupt the festivities. We followed slowly behind at a comfortable distance bringing up the rear of the wedding party.

Once again driving one lane, sometimes gravel roads, we were able to find the restaurant without trouble. It was a beautiful setting though there were no signs of life. Walking around the property peaking in windows, we found it deserted. I checked my phone to confirm I had the right time and day. I was surprised to find an email sent late the previous evening cancelling the reservation without explanation. Frustrated and in the middle of nowhere, we scrambled for a back-up plan. That afternoon, we planned to visit the Chateau de Commarque about a twenty-minute drive away. The nearest, decent sized town was Les Eyzies. As it was already ten past noon, I drove, and Courtney quickly scanned The Fork app for restaurants that had openings for lunch and found one called Nosco.

We drove fifteen minutes to Les Eyzies. In the Vézère valley, Les

Eyzies is known as the World Capital of Pre-History. The valley contains more than 150 known pre-historic sites, fifteen designated as UNESCO World Heritage Sites. One of them is the world-famous Lascaux cave and its paintings. We planned to skip this site as you can only tour a replica of the cave. The original cave is closed to the public to prevent further deterioration. We instead had followed our friend Stu's advice and had reservations for a tour of real cave paintings at Pech Merle later in the trip. Not knowing much about the town of Les Eyzies, we were impressed by the pretty village built below a cliff with visible caves high above. There was a highly rated prehistoric museum, but it was closed. Looking for the restaurant, we mistakenly drove down a pedestrian street. We were able to extricate ourselves and find public parking still presenting to Nosco on time.

At Nosco, the welcome was formal—not rude but not exactly warm either. We scored a small table on the terrasse and perused the menu. During lunch, we again saw several other parties get turned away despite an abundance of tables. We felt lucky to have procured one on such short notice. I had a wild mushroom starter, and Courtney ordered our only escargot of the trip (served in edible pastry shells). I once again went with Vin de Noix. We decided to finish off the light lunch with a charcuterie board. While we waited for our food, we planned the afternoon. Stu had recommended Chateau de Commarque as well. In addition, I had just finished a *Bruno* novel where this castle was the main setting. In the mystery, the assailant had hidden in an unnamed pre-historic cave across the valley before making his way to the castle to commit a murder. I studied nearby caves on Google Maps. I found one with five-star reviews. The comments sang its praises, describing personal tours of one of the few remaining privately owned caves led by quirky family members. You had to call personally to make "reservations." I suggested trying to arrange an early afternoon tour of the cave, which was on the way to the castle.

I stepped away from the table and down the alley to attempt the call.

The number rang so many times I almost hung up. Someone finally answered in a high pitched, sing-song voice. I wasn't sure if I was talking to a man or a woman. I asked if the cave was open today; it was. I then asked if we could tour around 2:30. "Ce n'est pas possible!" was the firm answer. I waited, not sure what to say. "Dix-sept heures [five pm], c'est d'accord?" the person continued after a pause. I thought quickly; we could tour the castle first and then back track to the cave. The person was focused on asking if I knew how to find the cave; he asked me twice. I assured him both times I could find it with my mapping program. And so, it was set. The food arrived at the table and this time it was just okay. Our grandmotherly friend would be happy to know that her Vin de Noix was far superior.

On our way to Commarque, we drove past the parking lot for the cave, so I felt assured that I could find my way back. Chateau de Commarque is a truly unique castle. It has a long history from three distinct periods—pre-history, troglodytic protohistory and the Middle Ages. The original portion of the castle was built on a rocky prominence in the twelfth century for the abbots of Sarlat. A number of independent noble houses were constructed on the grounds. Later due to the Hundred Years' War, defensive ramparts were built circling the entire compound for protection. Over time, the Beynac and the Commarque families became major rivals for power in the area. The Beynacs ended up taking control of the castle before it was eventually abandoned in the sixteenth century following the Wars of Religion. It fell into ruin over the next four hundred years. Brambles and dense vegetation grew to completely cover the entire site. It was rediscovered and listed as an historic monument in 1942. Since 1962, the current owner, Hubert de Commarque, has tirelessly supported its unearthing and restoration. Archeologic projects have led to fantastic discoveries.

The parking area was about a kilometer from the castle. It was a long walk in the woods on uneven ground unkind to my nagging hip. We eventually made it, hot and out of breath. We started at its base, walking around the outside of its impressive facade. Just below the base of the hill, troglodyte dwellings were restored and open for viewing. The caves were decorated with typical implements of daily protohistoric living. The prehistoric cave paintings were not open to the public, given a narrow and unstable entrance. Later, inside the castle, there was a video presentation and exhibits of the cave paintings found deep within the rocky outcropping. After viewing the outbuildings, we entered and toured the remains of the castle. Each of our visits to castles provided very different experiences, this one especially so. Many parts left in ruin, the restoration was far less polished than Castelnaud or Beynac (which we visited the following day). This lent it a mystical, rugged, authentic feel. You almost expected ghosts from centuries past to appear around every corner. To top it off, the commanding views from the top of the keep were majestic and marvelous. We were glad we made the trip. Despite being mostly downhill, the walk back to the car in the heat seemed much longer than a kilometer.

We drove back to the unpaved parking area for Bernifal cave arriving thirty minutes early. We were the only car in the large lot. There was a rundown building off to the side that I assumed must be near the cave entrance. I got out to read the covered bulletin board which confirmed we were in the right place but had no directions to the actual cave. As it had already been a long hot day, we stayed in the car with the air conditioning on to stay cool. Courtney decided to take a quick nap. While she was napping, I read through the reviews of the cave more carefully. A few reviews mentioned the cave was actually a ten-to-twenty-minute walk from the parking lot. It was now 4:40. I woke Courtney and told her we had to hurry.

We ducked through a clearing in the trees looking for directions. There was a rough path, actually more of an animal trail. There were no signs, but it was the only route we could see. It had to be the correct direction, right? A couple hundred meters into the forest, it became dark and spooky, gnarled trees leaning over the path at bizarre angles.

The Dordogne, also known as the Périgord, is divided into four regions named by color according to their landscape. For example, Périgord Vert is named for its lush greenery and Périgord Poupre for its grapes and vineyards. We were in the Périgord Noir (black) named for its dense forests and ever-present, dark oak trees. The dim forest added an air of mystery; it felt like we were in a scary, real life Hans Christian Andersen fairy tale. After another hundred meters, we finally saw a small sign roughly cut from thin plastic with the words, "Grotte de Bernifal," written in faded Sharpie with a script reminiscent of grade school penmanship. We looked at each other, shaking our heads. Were we really doing this? As we proceeded deeper into the forest, there was no sound and no sign of civilization. Like breadcrumbs in our fairy tale, we followed the make-shift handwritten signs… "Allez à La Grotte" [this way to the cave] with an arrow showing the way. Hurrying so as not to be late, we followed the last sign up a steep incline to a locked metal door carved into an overhang. There was a sign in French that appeared to list the rules of the cave though most of the words had faded such that it could not be read. We had made it by 4:50, but nowhere could the person with the high-pitched voice be found.

We waited in this isolated spot, and we waited. Five o'clock came and went; no one showed. Courtney kept asking if I should call. I hesitated not wanting to be a pain. Some of the reviews mentioned the owners were not always timely. At 5:10 though, I did call, and it again rang endlessly before eventually going to voice mail. We wondered if we were being stood up and considered leaving. At 5:15, a scooter pulled up and stopped at the base of the incline. It wasn't clear whether it was a man or a woman. The rider dismounted, helmet still on. Without waving, the person walked away from us to pee in the woods. Courtney whispered under her breath fears of a serial killer. Having relieved himself, he now removed his helmet to reveal a funny little man waving with a smile. In no hurry, he ambled up the path with a large backpack. Seeing the heavy bag, Courtney repeated her whispered fear.

"Hellooo!" he called out in a high-pitched British accent. He introduced himself as Michael. He put his bag down and fumbled through it for a full minute before turning his attention to us. He launched into a rehearsed history of the cave and his family. The Magdelenian cave was discovered in 1902 on his family's property. The Magdalenian period denotes the final Paleolithic period lasting from 17,000 to 11,500 years ago. Archeologists have extensively studied more than one hundred cave paintings and interesting tectiform symbols found within Grotte de Bernifal. Tectiform symbols have been found here and in numerous other prehistoric caves (fifty-two in Europe by one source). Thirty-two geometric shapes are repeated extensively in these caves. Though archeologists have not been able to decipher them, they obviously carry meaning. These symbols are felt to be precursors in the development of more complicated communication.

Michael's uncle, Gilbert Pémendrant, who per past reviews was also quite a character, had been instrumental in the promotion and further exploration of the cave. A cult classic documentary, *Le Dernier Paysan Prehistorien* [The Last Peasant Farmer, Pre-Historian], was filmed about his remarkable passion for the cave. Unfortunately, M. Pémendrant passed away in 2007, and I have not been able to locate a copy of this film (despite extensive online searching). Gilbert was eager to share his family's cave with others and personally led intimate tours of the complex well into his eighties. Michael continues his uncle's tradition (and his passion).

As Michael proceeded with his high-pitched lecture, I studied him. He was dressed in working man's clothing but with a peculiar, eccentric flare. He had no upper teeth. He was a quirky little man but was an absolute savant when it came to the cave. His engaging style made you smile as did some of the errors in his English which was overall quite good. His British accent added to the entertaining presentation. The sing-songy intonations seemed as if cut from an episode of Monty Python's Flying Circus. You couldn't help becoming absorbed and giggling along with Michael's animated tale.

He ended his speech ceremoniously, and with a flashlight in one hand and a key held high in the other, declared dramatically, "And now we enter the cave!" I asked if pictures were allowed without a flash (they are not in most pre-historic caves). "Pictures okay (voice rising), flash or no flash!" he exclaimed. The cave had no lighting, so when he closed the door behind us, it was pitch black save the flashlight which began to sputter. Shaking the flashlight, he cursed battery life and asked us to wait right there. Leaving us twenty-five meters into the cave, he returned to the door and left, closing it behind him. Courtney was now convinced we weren't making it out alive! After a few moments in the kind of dark one can only find in a cavern of this sort, the door reopened to our relief. He returned with a new flashlight and a long laser pointer.

As I sit here contemplating how to describe what followed, it is clear this was yet another experience on the trip that words simply cannot do justice. The cave paintings were absolutely mind blowing, an awe-inspiring adventure back in time. Unfortunately, the pictures we took do not accurately depict the vivid and vibrant paintings. The paintings were spread out over four caverns. The detailed, whirlwind explanations provided by Michael made it hard to process and remember all the details he shared. He outlined, with his laser pointer, figures that were hard to discern. He was well versed in the chemistry behind the different paints used, going on sidebar discussions of magnesium, iron oxide, and other compounds used in the various colored paints. As a chemistry major, it made perfect sense to me in the moment, though at points, it felt like he was freelancing a little. However, later in the trip, a professional cave guide repeated facts almost identical to Michael's. He explained which of the paintings had disputed interpretations amongst various archeologists. Furthermore, he was knowledgeable in explaining the geology of the cave. The geologic features in the four caverns were magnificent in their own right. Michael was pleased to report, the cave had been listed as a UNESCO World Heritage Site in 1979 and that the former French president, François Mitterrand, had made a trip to visit.

So how to describe the actual paintings? This is the hard part. Michael explained the paintings and artifacts found in the cave have been dated to a wide-ranging period of time—the oldest 35,000 years old and the youngest 13,000. Represented on the walls were bison, ibex, fish, horses, and mammoths, among others. One painting represented a bear with tally marks next to it, felt to represent how many bears the artist had killed. Another depicted a bison with red marks painted at certain key locations. These have been interpreted as a visual manual of sorts passing down knowledge on how to make the kill. Yet another painting depicted a series of marks on a line that appeared to represent a landscape. Michael explained that archeologists have been able to map each line to corresponding caves and places of safety nearby—a caveman's Google Maps! One last painting of note has been interpreted, alternatively, as either a fish or a house (which sounds weird though it really depended on which of the faded lines your eyes followed). They solved this mystery with new technology that allowed them to blow up and project the image on the cave floor. Archeologists counted more than a thousand separate stick spots (brush strokes) in what was in reality a tiny image, maybe six inches in diameter. The controversy was settled, and the painting was declared a fish. One more astounding fact to remember is that all of this art was drawn in the dark by torch light.

Probably the most humorous moment of the visit occurred when we approached the fourth cavern which was located just beyond a steep and slippery slope. With Michael explaining how we were going to proceed, I took a video with my phone that we will cherish forever. In his best Monty Python voice, Michael explained:

"We are going to the fourse room and for the fourse room... we are going down. I go down first and then I will be here [flashing his light far down the incline]. You wait and I will light you and then you go down. And you go with me... [He starts down] You put your hand here to break... [when he can't think of the word, I offer 'fall'], yes! You push your the side. One time! [He reaches to the wall for stability] I do it myself, six times. [He starts carefully down the slope] Second time, [voice rising as he reaches for the next hand-hold] sshird time, fours time, fif time, seex time. And now it is good. I am very comp-ee-tant [turning to shine his light to guide us down]."

The most extraordinary site of the cave was actually in the first cavern but definitely deserves its own paragraph. On a projection of rock that roughly approximated the head of a person, a talented pre-historic artist had painted a sublime face of a woman. Michael explained that the painting had been dated to 16,000 years. It was eerie. It was magical. It was a little haunting. Right there peering out from a cave wall was a woman's face with thoughtful eyes, inquisitive eyebrows, black hair, and a small pretty mouth. Her features stared out at you as if she was contemplating her own look into the future. Standing there mesmerized, it felt like you were communing with a fellow human being. It was as if you knew her—understood her thoughts, her hopes, her desires. It is an image that will forever be burned into our collective memory.

Tracing our way back to the entrance door, we exited to what felt like blinding sunlight despite the deep shadows of the dense forest. After having spent an hour and forty-five minutes with us, Michael gathered himself with a deep breath and said, "I will collect my eight euros now"—the price of admission. An unbelievable personal tour of one of the most spectacular sites we have ever visited for eight euros! We thanked him for the exceptional tour. He formally wished us a good vacation and promptly marched back down the incline, mounted his scooter, and left us standing alone in the forest...

We drove back to Sarlat alternating between stunned silence and animated discussion of what we had just experienced. We cooked a vegetarian dinner from our market haul—three types of mushrooms, fresh shallots, and garlic sauteed in Brittany butter and again deglazed with sweet Monbazillac wine. Courtney made a nice salad with the perfectly ripe ancienne tomatoes. Washed down with a cold rosé followed by a vintage Armagnac digestif, it was perfect. We considered going out on the town but decided to stay in and, with only two days left on the trip, do a little pre-packing. Later in bed, I think we both fell asleep contemplating the kind face of the Paleolithic woman staring out at us from the ether.

22

AM I CATHOLIC?

We had planned to be up early for the seventy-minute drive to Rocamadour, a site of religious pilgrimage which has become a tourist magnet. Our internet friend, Stu, recommended getting there by 9am at the latest. He suggested touring the town and leaving by late morning before the legions of tourists descended. From there, we planned to drive part way back to a highly rated restaurant in Souillac where I had made a reservation for 12:30. However, after another night of being up past midnight, the trip had finally caught up to us. We decided to sleep in and go to Rocamadour late in the day. We did get up in time to visit Château de Beynac closer to home. With a quick visit there, we could make it to Souillac by 12:30 for lunch then proceed on to Rocamadour for an afternoon visit.

Château de Beynac was one of the few "flex" activities left on our list. In actuality, we were both prepared to skip it, given we had already toured two medieval castles. We had already seen Château de Beynac from the water, from the hanging gardens of Marqueyssac and from the competing Château de Castelnaud. Those views were all superb, but nothing compared to viewing the foreboding structure up close. The man at the ticket booth complimented our French then broke into his own proud English to explain the audio guide. The guide was very well done and easy to use. It covered the history in a very complete way and, left to my own devices, I would have listened to all fifty clips. Unfortunately, we were on a bit of a time schedule, so we had to be efficient.

We started outside, taking in the view from the cliff overlooking a bend in the Dordogne River. You could see why the site was such a strategic stronghold. The views were breathtaking. From the overlook we could see canoes and gabarres tracing our path down the river from earlier in the week. Unlike Castelnaud which was set up like a museum, Beynac was filled with authentic furnishings and period pieces. There was an opulent, spiral staircase and panoramic views from the top of the keep. One of the highlights was Richard the Lionheart's fully furnished bedroom.

The castle was built in the twelfth century by the Barons of Beynac. With trade increasing, the gabarres carrying local goods had to acquire a rite of passage from the Lord of Beynac. Controlling the river route, therefore, was very lucrative. Adhémar de Beynac participated in the Second Crusade from 1146 to 1148. When he died without an heir in 1194, the castle passed into the hands of Richard the Lionheart who was instrumental in the Third Crusade. At that time, Richard was the King of England as well as the Duke of both Normandy and Aquitaine. During the Hundred Years' War, Beynac was back in French hands, though like many towns and castles in the area, it was passed back and forth with the fortunes of war.

Toward the end of the self-guided tour, there were several interesting features and exhibits. In the dining room for the troops, there were long tables with holes cut in their ends to hold swords during dinner. Nearby, on display in open air were the actual helmet and shield used by the Baron of Beynac during the Third Crusade. But, probably my favorite part of the castle was the fascinating sally port with multiple lines of defense which made taking the castle nearly impossible. First, attackers would have to cross a moat and drawbridge to get to the only entrance to the castle. The sally port was a long, narrow rectangular space. The exterior door was reinforced with iron such that it could not be burnt through. Then, should troops actually make it into the sally port, the rectangular space had a balcony with a defensive wall containing arrow slots and places where hot pitch could be dropped on the invaders. Finally, there was a second, retractable inner door which, when open, served as a bridge over a snake-filled pit of water. When attacked, the door would be pulled up and locked tight. Thus, in addition to dodging arrows and hot pitch, the opposing army would also have to contend with a snake filled pit of Indiana Jones proportions. Thankfully, there are no longer snakes in the pit! As a final parting goodbye, when we exited, there was a man in period dress playing medieval music on an ancient instrument we'd never before seen.

When we made it back to the car, Google maps showed our arrival in Souillac as 12:25. Navigating through the ever-present roundabouts, we only made one brief wrong turn on our way. We arrived right on time. Getting out to look for our restaurant, Souillac immediately felt different. It had a rough, edgy feel and the grit that we loved in Arles during our first trip to France. It took us a minute to find our restaurant, and for the second time on our trip, our reserved restaurant was CLOSED. I wasn't sure whether to be angry at the restaurant or myself for my lack of skill in making reservations. We walked back to the main road where we had seen a restaurant with a full terrasse.

Using Courtney's "follow the locals—people vote with their feet" theory, we walked up to Crêperie Salé Sucrépes and asked if they had a table. They did if we didn't mind sitting inside. As we sat down, we received the, now common, furrowed brow and curious glances from the other diners. Once again, it was clear that we "weren't from here." Ours were the only non-French voices in the restaurant, and the wait staff spoke absolutely no English. But as we found nearly everywhere, once we broke out the French, we were welcomed like honored visitors.

We went with a "hot day rosé." I ordered a galette topped with a large duck breast cooked in walnut oil. On top of the duck was melting Rocamadour goat cheese and tomato confit. Courtney's galette was chicken with Emmental cheese, mushrooms, and mustarde ancienne. Both were outstanding. I finished with a dessert crêpe with caramelized apples and salted butter caramel. Sometimes the best meals are the ones that are unexpected. Sluggish after three weeks of nearly non-stop touring, I definitely needed coffee and ordered my usual "un double." Courtney, on the other hand, made one of our few faux pas of the trip. She attempted to order a café crème (which of course can only be consumed at breakfast). The young waitress stopped dead in her tracks and actually had to ask the senior waitress if it was allowed. They forgave our foreignness and served Courtney her café crème anyway!

Not having researched Souillac beyond a stopping point for lunch, I read about the town as we ate. We decided to walk down and visit what turned out to be a famous cathedral. On our way, we passed what is left of the former Church of Saint Martin. After being ravaged by Protestants in the Wars of Religion and later by a fire, all that remains is a tall belfry that now serves as a clock tower in the center of town. What remains still shows the scars of the fire and now houses l'Office de Tourisme. The clock tower is an impressive site, but the jewel of the city is clearly the twelfth century Benedictine abbey around the corner.

Abbatiale-Saint-Marie is one of the best examples of Romanesque and Byzantine architecture in southwestern France. Laid out in a Latin cross design, the sanctuary was inspired by the church of Hagia Sophia in Istanbul. The exterior is notable for three successive domes. The interior is decorated with several masterpieces of sculpture. The most famous is a carving of Isaiah which is considered one of the most important depictions of the prophet in all of Romanesque art. Another carved pillar caught my attention; it illustrated the wages of sin with many fabulous beasts, one of which was eating a man at the very top. Along one side of the church were empty stone sarcophagi dating to the eighth and ninth centuries which were discovered during repair work on the tower's porch. The altar under the domed apse consisted of a simple, solitary statue of Mary. The quiet, austere atmosphere added to the ancient feel of the building. Though we had not planned on visiting, it ended up being one of the most interesting churches we saw. All in all, our quick visit to Souillac was extremely high yield. We left with nothing but good feelings for the place.

We now set off on pilgrimage to Rocamadour. In his internet guide to the Dordogne, Stu had described in detail how the parking situation was a nightmare. The three-level town had limited space, and one option to avoid was the lot far down in the valley which required catching "Le Petit Train" up to the lower village. Stu suggested going early and snagging one of the few public spots in a small lot just west of town. With our arrival timed for mid to late afternoon, I hoped we might luck out if we mapped to "that" parking area on Google Maps. Absentmindedly, I accidentally selected the next "parking" symbol over—about a kilometer or two off given the scale of the map. I set off proud of my insider information that would surely score us a primo parking space.

As mentioned in my driving tips, every crossroads in France has small, labeled signs pointing to the closest town in each direction. As we got closer to our "destination," Google would tell me to turn right when the Rocamadour sign pointed left and vice versa. I continued to follow Google certain I was taking a backroads shortcut. When we turned down a deeply rutted, dirt road, Courtney questioned my sanity. Testing the strength of the shocks and struts, I was glad we were in a rental car. Hoping that the dirt path would miraculously give way onto a small parking lot with one shining open spot, I reached a dead end, really just a dirt space. We were definitely at "a" parking lot. However, from the cars and vans loaded with gear, we appeared to be in the parking area for a camping location. Going back to the mapping app, I realized that although only a kilometer or two away, we were in the next valley over. The only way to proceed was to drive back out of this valley and around to Rocamadour adding an additional twenty minutes.

Flustered by my mistake, I frantically tried to map us back. I don't think clearly when flustered. Without having been to Rocamadour before, it was hard to visualize how a 3-D, three-level town appears on a two-dimensional map (it just appears to be a series of parallel roads despite the top level rising five hundred feet above the canyon). In haste to fix my error, I now incorrectly mapped us to a parking lot on the highest level. To get there required hair pin turns going straight up in the middle of a traffic jam. When I finally saw a clearing and parking spaces alongside the road, I grabbed the first one I could. I was relieved to be at least somewhere near our intended destination. What I didn't know was that I had parked across from the Chapelle de l'Hospitalet, a thirteenth century Romanesque church. Pilgrims stopped here for centuries to rest and receive medical attention before walking the additional mile or so to the pilgrimage site.

Rocamadour is yet another UNESCO World Heritage site and is on "The Way of St. James" pilgrim route. Clinging to a steep cliff rising out of a canyon, the village is an absolutely staggering site. If you can suspend judgment for a bit, its long history is a fantastic tale filled with legends and miracles. The story begins in the fourth century when a man named Amadour chose this spot as a religious hermitage. Legend has it that he was actually Zacchaeus from the Bible who had to flee the Holy Lands to escape persecution (never mind that the dates don't add up by at least a century or two). Though pilgrims had already started to travel to the site before the year 1000, it was in 1166 that a perfectly preserved body was found in a stone sarcophagus. It was felt to be the body of Amadour who had died centuries before.

In 1172, a book, the *Livre des Miracles* was written, documenting the mystical healing power of the site. Pilgrims and penitents began to travel from afar dressed in robes adorned with crosses. On arrival to

Rocamadour, they would strip off their robes and climb the 223 steps of the "Via Sancta" to pray for miracles in front of the Black Madonna. Famous pilgrims who made the trip include Henry Plantagenet, Elanor of Aquitaine, St. Bernard, St. Louis, and his mother Blanche of Castille to name a few. Stop me if you have heard this one, but the site suffered damage in both the Hundred Years' War and the Wars of Religion. After being sacked by Protestants, only the twelfth century statue of the Virgin Mary, *The Black Madonna*, and a ninth century bell survived. The site was rebuilt. There are now eight separate chapels on the cliff ledge which makes up the middle level of the village. On the top level, a castle can be found, built to protect the religious sites along with "The Cross of Jerusalem" brought to Rocamadour by pilgrims from Palestine.

One other fanciful legend of Rocamdour concerns the knight immortalized in "The Song of Roland," one of the first great "Chansons de Geste" (epic lyrical poems performed by troubadours). Roland was a knight and the nephew of Charlemagne. His famous sword was named "Durendal" (from the French word durer—to endure). It was a gift from Charlemagne himself. In 788, at the Battle of Roncevaux Pass in the Pyrenees, Roland is said to have held off 100,000 Saracens (Moors) with his sword in a rear-guard operation. In one version, mortally wounded, he uses his sword to slash through the mountains so he could see France one last time before he died. This mountain pass is named La Brèche de Roland (Roland's Gap). Reflecting on how many battles he won with his invincible sword, near death, he decided it could not fall into the hands of the Moors. From the Song of Roland:

"I would rather die than have it remain with the pagans. God our Father do not let France be dishonored in this way."

He unsuccessfully tried to destroy the sword which would not break. He instead threw it, and with the divine assistance of the Archangel

Michael, the sword traveled several hundred kilometers in the air to embed itself in the rock cliff high above Rocamadour where it can still be seen today.

So, back to the pilgrim "hospital." At the time, we still didn't realize we were nearly a mile away. Nevertheless, it was actually a good place to start. The cliff face curves gradually around to l'Hospitalet area. The vantage point provided a great photo op with Rocamadour rising in profile vertically out of the valley. We started our walk following the signs pointing to the castle and chapel areas. It was another brutally hot day. My hip pain was raging, but with just one day left, I wasn't giving up now. We walked past the upper most terminal of the "Ascenseur" which like the funiculaire at Montmartre was a large elevator car on an inclined plane.

At the end of our long walk was the castle built to protect the city. You could go in and climb the ramparts for two euros each. It was an unmanned, coin operated entrance. We each deposited our coins and went in. The ramparts were accessed by a stairway that hung out over the valley far below. Excited, I walked to the top before turning to see Courtney in the fetal position, hyperventilating, about ten steps up. Never one for heights, she just couldn't do it. I went back and helped her down, and she waited while I climbed back up for some absolutely amazing vistas. It wasn't crowded at all. I was one of two people on the ramparts. At least at 4pm on a June day, the crowds were nowhere to be found. It felt like being alone on top of the world.

Rather than walk down the stairs to the chapel level, we took the Ascenseur purchasing "aller-retour" tickets to get there and back. Arriving at the middle level and passing through the gate, there were ancient chapels in every direction. We started with the Chapel of Notre Dame which houses the Black Madonna. The highlighted black sculpture was the centerpiece of the solemn chapel. Maybe it is just the legend that surrounds her, but she almost appeared alive. Heads bowed, there were many in intense, silent prayer. On the walls, there were centuries old stone tablets listing all the verified miracles attributed to the Black

Madonna. I took some pictures then sat down and thought, "What the heck?" In a moment of silence, I asked for a cure of my hip pain, a constant companion on the trip.

Outside the chapel of the Black Madonna, there was an empty stone coffin in a nook with a sign indicating this was Amadour's actual casket found in 1166. It now served as a receptacle for wish coins. I added a euro, again asking for my hip to be healed. Next, we sought The Sword of Roland. We had to look hard, and many who visit likely miss it, but about seventy-five feet up, just outside the chapel, the Sword of Roland was embedded in the cliff face. I later read that the "actual," original sword has been moved to the Cluny Museum in Paris. Thus, the sword I was marveling over was, in reality, just a replica—so much for my brush with the Archangel Michael!

Many of the chapels were interconnected, and each was a little different. The Chapel of St. John the Baptist celebrated the famous historical figures who had come here on pilgrimage. One chapel miraculously smelled of pizza. We figured out later an Italian restaurant must be somewhere below in the lower village. The most bizarre chapel, though, was the Chapelle de l'Ovalie which for some peculiar reason is dedicated to rugby. Jerseys of famous, presumably Christian, rugby players lined the wall. The main altar had an unusual modern figure of Mary praying with a well-built, naked man facing her, also in prayer. The idol had been donated by "Les Amis de Notre Dame du Rugby." This unexpected sight was a humorous highlight for me.

We made our way back to the Ascenseur and rode it to the upper level of the town. For the first five minutes of our walk returning to the car, I had absolutely zero hip pain. Because the pain had come and gone during the trip, I wondered if this was a coincidence or if the Black Madonna had truly performed another miracle. I walked another hundred yards without pain. For a minute, I considered converting. Then, about halfway to the car, the hip pain came roaring back. I looked at Courtney and declared, "I guess I'm not Catholic."

The drive home was uneventful. We ate a tasty home-cooked dinner using up our leftovers and savored the end of our trip by finishing off the bottle of 1989 Delord Armagnac we had been working on since Gascony. We decided to venture out in the dark to see Sarlat one last time. We were in search of ice cream. Everything except bars was pretty much closed. We did find one ice cream stand that was just starting to clean-up for the night. I asked if they might be willing to serve one more customer and got a flat, "Non." I guess you can't have everything. We took some final pictures of Sarlat and said our goodbyes to the beautiful city.

THE DAY FRANCE TOLD
US TO GO HOME: A VERY
LONG GOODBYE

W e had booked timed tickets for the first tour of the cave paintings at Pech Merle. It was an hour-and-a-half away and in the general direction of Toulouse where we had hotel reservations at the airport for an early departure the next morning. We would have to leave Sarlat early to make it to Pech Merle. We had reservations for lunch in nearby Saint-Cirq-Lapopie (one of Stu's favorite French villages) before driving on to Toulouse to drop off the rental. The United States was still requiring travelers to test negative for COVID-19 within twenty-four hours of departure. We planned to complete remote testing from the hotel. The Air France, Delta rideshare flight from Toulouse would take us to Paris Charles de Gaulle (CDG) where after a long layover, we'd fly Delta to the United States. Despite a lot of moving parts, it seemed like the perfect plan to get something out of our last day and still be ready to catch our early AM flight out of Toulouse.

For all of the Delta flights to France, both coming and going, I had confirmed seats when I first booked. For the Air France ride-share flight from Toulouse (TLS), confirming seats was not an option. After seeing so many people bumped from the flight from Atlanta to Paris, we wanted to check-in first thing that morning to claim our seats. This seemed especially important as the travel industry was still in complete chaos as it tried to recover from the pandemic. Given past experiences of getting bumped, delayed, and even stranded, I always get a little nervous prior to a travel day. Nevertheless, I started the morning fairly relaxed since we were up in plenty of time to check-in before making our drive to Pech Merle.

Drinking my morning coffee while Courtney showered, I first tried to check-in through the Delta site. This didn't work; the site simply referred to the flight from TLS as a partnered Air France flight. Moving to the Air France website didn't solve the problem; the site was an endless loop. Using combinations of the reservation code and flight number, I could identify our flight but trying to check-in simply kicked me back to the original screen. Now I was getting nervous. I found the Air France customer service number (in English) and tried to call. Calling shortly after seven o'clock, I reached a recording stating operating hours began at 8am. I was able to direct message a Delta rep through their app and explained our predicament. The return message assured me they could get me checked in. After going back and forth several times, I got the message, "Oh, you'll have to talk to a representative in Toulouse." As we didn't plan to be in Toulouse until evening, this message did not help to quell my anxiety. But now we were running late for Pech Merle. I showered quickly then hurried to pack the car and get on the road.

Our tickets for Pech Merle were for 9:45 with strict instruction that you must arrive thirty minutes early or risk missing your tour. As we left Sarlat, Google Maps showed our arrival time as 9:46. Now I was not only nervous about checking-in but fairly certain we'd miss the cave. After 8am, Courtney repeatedly tried the English number for Air France. Somewhere along the way, we realized the English number was meant for people in America where it was now about 2am! She switched over to trying the French number for Air France. That number was answered with a message in rapid French neither of us could understand after which it hung up. We decided we'd have to get to Toulouse as soon as we could after the cave and talk to an agent on-site. We were not sure how our perfect plan for the day had gone haywire so quickly!

I was pushing the speed limit as much as I could on the twisting rural roads trying my best to slow down for anything that appeared to be a roadside speed box. Courtney was already a little nauseous before we left. The wild ride didn't help and made her a little cranky. With my speeding, I had cut our arrival time down to 9:41. Google Maps, which had worked so well for most of the trip, now became delayed in giving directions. Because of this, we took a wrong turn. By the time we were back on track, even a 9:45 arrival was in jeopardy. Speeding toward our destination, the road narrowed and took sweeping curves around steep drop-offs with no guardrails. Courtney was now flat out ill and a little green around the gills.

We pulled into the parking lot of Pech Merle at precisely 9:44. We literally ran from the parking lot to rush the woman sitting behind the check-in desk. Just as we stepped to the desk, her phone rang. She gave us a disdainful look before turning her head, as if she hadn't seen us, and answered the call. As I stood teetering back and forth with restless anxiety, she slowly and deliberately handled the call. She finally hung up and returned her gaze to us with a piercing stare. Without a beat I said, "Bonjour, Madame. Je suis vraiment desolé! Nous sommes en retard." At the French apology, she softened and said, "Pas de problème," handing me two tickets and pointing us toward a group outside the cave entrance. In retrospect, we both think she was ready to gleefully tell us we were too late until we made our apology. Hurrying to the group, the guide literally started talking as we approached.

Pech Merle is one of the few caves where you can still enter and view the original paintings. The number of visitors allowed per day is tightly regulated. Our group contained about twenty-five people, and we were given earpieces so we could all hear the guide's presentation. The professional guide started her smooth but somewhat canned talk by apologizing that it would only be in French. We were given a laminated booklet in English with a brief description of each highlighted exhibit. We were shown a short video presentation in French before entering the cave. As we entered, our guide explained that pictures of any kind were expressly forbidden.

Pech Merle is an extraordinary site. The paintings were discovered in 1922 by three teenagers. The cave has been fully explored and re-searched. It was classified an historic monument in 1952. The caverns were created by an underground river about two million years ago, later to be used by humans for shelter. Over eight hundred separate artistic expressions have been identified, many depicting animals. The murals and pictures are of varying ages with the oldest dating back 29,000 years.

The cave paintings at Pech Merle are, without a doubt, stunning. They are definitely more vivid and dramatic than those at Grotte de Bernifal. But, after our quirky, intimate tour of the latter, Pech Merle felt a little "Disney-fied." This is not to say I wouldn't recommend Pech Merle to others. It is definitely a site to behold. However, being herded along carefully constructed sidewalks with guard rails while the guide switched on professional lighting before starting her scripted talk just wasn't the same experience as a personal tour lit only by Michael's flash-light (and his contagious enthusiasm). I do understand that limiting the number of visitors, minimizing light exposure, and keeping guests well clear of the paintings are all designed to prevent damage to the cave. Damage caused by visitors is why the famous Lascaux cave paintings are now only viewable in a replica cave. At Pech Merle, our group was too large for us all to see each wall at the same time. At each stop, the guide would give her spiel twice as people in each half-group jockeyed for the best viewing position before being moved along to the next room. We could pick out phrases in her French presentation but mostly relied on the scanty descriptions in our English pamphlet to interpret the paintings.

The first set of paintings is referred to as *The Black Frieze*. On this wall are depicted twenty-five different animals including horses, mammoths, bison, and a type of antelope. At another point, there is a bear artistically carved into the wall. Taking us around the corner, the guide directed our attention to the ceiling. High above our heads could be seen a painting of a mammoth and also a fertility figure. These representations of buxom women are common for the era and can be found in numerous caves across Europe. The cave had some interesting geologic features as well, including several perfectly round "pearl" formations. Next to come was a footprint left in muddy substrate centuries ago, now preserved and mineralized. Research on the print has determined it was left by a twelve-year-old boy some 12,000 years ago. There were several "negative" handprints throughout the cave. These were produced by the artist placing his hand against the wall while blowing powdered pigment to stain the outline of the hand. Seeing such tangible evidence of the real people behind the art was awesome and a little humbling. We finished our tour with the most striking (and famous) painting—*The Spotted Horses*. Giant in scale, the two horses are painted back-to-back and are exquisitely decorated with black dots. Scientists have debated whether the placement of these dots confers meaning or if they are simply an accurate representation of the horses that lived at the time. Near the painting is a human handprint which is felt to be the artist's signature.

Finished with the tour, we decided to skip the museum so we could get to Toulouse to see about getting checked-in and confirmed on our flight. We had planned to stop at our last of "Les Plus Beaux Villages de France," Saint-Cirq-Lapopie, on the way to Toulouse. It was highly recommended by Stu and has previously been voted "France's favorite village." It was about a fifteen-minute drive from Pech Merle, and we had made reservations for lunch well ahead of time. Since it was on our way and we had to eat somewhere, we decided not to skip Saint-Cirq-Lapopie which turned out to be a great decision.

Parking was reported to be problematic in this steep, cliffside village. I targeted the lot closest to the town to minimize walking more hills. Confidently, I mapped us to this location. It was an easy drive until we approached the bridge over the Lot River. Though only a few kilometers in distance further, we could see the town overlooking the valley atop a three-hundred-foot sheer, limestone cliff. Those last kilometers were going to be straight up. Traversing increasingly narrow switchbacks, we made it to the main street above the village. It was a narrow two-lane road with no sidewalks pinned between tight guard rails. Google had been slow all morning. Nearing the parking area, it told me, at the very last second, to turn sharply left, so I did. Taking the hairpin left and going straight up, I couldn't see around the corner. The road was blocked to through traffic with concrete barriers. Now turned sideways and blocking both lanes of the main road, I was once again flustered. A really pissed French driver blocked by my car started honking manically. As I tried to back down out of the way, he raced around my backside nearly hitting me. He gunned his engine while treating me to a rude hand gesture.

Once I got to a place where I could pull over, I tried to map the back roads to find the entrance to that lot (which you could actually see just beyond the concrete barriers). A recurring theme today, Google once again failed me. I was directed on an eight-minute wild goose chase that, like the day before, left me on a dirt road—this time outside a farmer's house. Studying the map and remembering signs we passed, we realized we were looking for the "Village" lot. Without Google, I backtracked to the turn off for the Village lot. Pleased with myself, I started to turn in only to find an RV completely blocking the only road there. It was not moving as if broken down. Completely giving up, we decided to park at the "P5" lot we had seen on one edge of town. At least it had plenty of empty spaces.

Getting out of the car, we didn't realize we had parked on the opposite end of town from our restaurant. It was eight hundred meters away which doesn't sound like much... if you don't take into account the topography. We could not walk directly to the town due to the narrow road with no sidewalks. We had to take a path up into the woods that wound steeply up and down. I wasn't sure my hip was going to make it to the end of the trip. Once in the city, the steep, cobbled roads were even harder to traverse. It was also another hot day; so, sweating through my shirt and pulling myself along with any handrail I could grab onto, we made our way slowly to the restaurant, our last true meal in France.

Despite all the chaos getting there, we walked onto the terrace of Le Cantou at 12:01 for our noon reservation. The staff spoke no English. Explaining we had a reservation and apologizing for our poor French worked well one last time. We again watched many other parties get turned away as our meal progressed. We decided to order opposite choices from the nineteen euro, three-course formula. My starter was a delicious Florentine Perfect Egg. Courtney started with gazpacho made from peas served in a wide water glass with a chunk of goat cheese artfully floating on top. A pichet of cold Bergerac white for eight euros was perfect for the warm day. My main dish was a highlight—lacquered Aveyron pork belly with horseradish and celery puree. Courtney had fish—a filet of Hake served with simmered soy beans floating in a bath of sage-flavored broth. For dessert, I went chocolate, of course, with two brownies served sandwich style with crème de praline in between. Courtney loved her "exotic verrine" with passion fruit mousse, mango tartare, and a tasty crumble. It was a fantastic last meal with delectable food and attentive, amiable service.

A little more relaxed after some wine and a nice lunch, we decided we had time to tour the town before heading to Toulouse. Saint-Cirq-Lapopie is a remarkable village. It was strategically built atop a cliff overlooking the Lot River valley. It was the main seat of Lapopie, one of four feudal dynasties that made up the Quercy region. Like almost every town in the area, it was touched by the Hundred Years' War and the Wars of Religion. Though not much of them is left, there are remains of three separate fortresses which topped the large hill at the edge of the cliff. The view back toward the village revealed layers of quaint thirteenth to sixteenth century buildings constructed of local yellow stone, some half-timbered and all topped with brown tiled roofs. Cobbled lanes unchanged since medieval times completed the picture. The village has long been a magnet for artists and writers and that tradition continues today with numerous studios and galleries. Co-founder of the Surrealist movement, the famous French writer and poet André Breton was particularly enamored with the village. He called it "an impossible rose in the night" and when he got to Saint-Cirq-Lapopie for the first time, he declared, "I no longer want to be anywhere else."

Exiting the restaurant, we hugged the edge of the cliff to circle the sixteenth century church which is the main feature in the skyline. It was built on the foundations of an earlier Roman temple. We walked past the ruins of one of the castles and despite the steep steps, climbed to the top of the largest hill. It was painful, but I made it. This spot afforded commanding, panoramic views of the Lot River valley far below. Saint-Cirq-Lapopie is within twenty-five kilometers of Cahors, home to one of our favorite French appellations. On our way back to the car, Courtney spotted a highly rated wine shop we had read about. We popped in and after proper French greetings explained to the woman that we were looking for a Cahors to drink today ("pour boire aujourd'hui"), our last night in France. She answered in very quick French in an accent that was new to us. We went back and forth before understanding that she was asking if we preferred a lighter version or one with a stronger, bolder taste. We indicated the latter. She took us directly to a bottle that ended up being the best bottle of Cahors we drank on the trip. She was insistent that it was to be opened for at least one to two hours before drinking, "Absolument!" The price was not marked, so I expected to pay through the teeth. When I got to the counter, I was surprised to find it was only fifteen euros.

Leaving Saint-Cirq-Lapopie, we had a two hour and fifteen-minute drive to the airport to drop the rental car. After three weeks on the go and with air conditioning on, Courtney took a well-deserved nap. The roads coming down out of the hills were fun, and with Courtney asleep, I was able to open it up on the winding arcs. Exiting the high country, we passed through a rural agricultural area. Google was definitely taking us the scenic route; some of the tiny roads were not much more than cow paths. We actually had to pass a tractor at one point. Also worn out by the string of consecutive long days, I was more than ready to ditch the car, confirm our airline seats, and get tucked into our hotel room early.

As we approached the outskirts of Toulouse, the traffic picked up. It had to have been rush hour. There was a traffic jam at a roundabout. As usual with multiple lane circles, the proper etiquette was unclear to me (as well as everyone else in the circle). For the second time on this day, a local driver laid on his horn hard, cussing me out. Later, swiftly moving traffic came to an immediate halt when unexpectedly a crossing guard stepped out in the road; school was out. After a day of nothing going right, my nerves were frazzled, and my knuckles began to ache from squeezing the wheel. To return the car full, I had mapped to the closest grocery store gas station, a Géant. Twice during the trip, I had filled up at Carrefour hypermarchés without incident. Pulling into the unmanned, twenty-four-hour pumps gave me a chance to catch my breath from the stress of heavy traffic. Getting out to fill the car, the Géant pumps rejected my American credit cards. This day!!!

I mapped to what appeared to be the closest Carrefour Market. What I didn't count on was it being on the other side of a river. We were directed an additional fifteen minutes up and over a bridge before heading back down to Carrefour. Now successfully gassed up and the only car at the multiple pump station, I tried to map to Europcar. As I was punching in the coordinates, a woman pulled up behind me and, you guessed it, laid on her horn. I am not sure why she couldn't have used one of the other four empty pumps! Part way there, Courtney suggested that maybe we could head to the hotel, which was actually inside the airport complex, and drop off our luggage before returning the car. This made perfect sense, so she re-mapped us to the hotel.

Close to the airport at a roundabout, Google directed us to take the third exit. I caught a quick glance at the schematic sign as we entered and thought I saw the word "interdit" (forbidden) next to our suggested exit. It was too late though as I blindly followed the guiding voice down the one-way road. A couple hundred meters later, we could actually see the hotel past a few alternating barriers. However, the only exit from the road was clearly meant for professional drivers only. A long line of town cars and limousines were backed up behind a guy in a mini-van who was stuck behind a traffic arm. I pulled over to the side behind the alternating barriers. The mini-van extricated itself from the line and drove over to me. The man rolled down his window and asked in French if he could exit by weaving through the barriers. I answered, "Je sais pas." (I don't know.) He said, "Regarde moi," (watch me) to see if he could get through. He traversed several barriers and then obviously hit a dead end. If I was frazzled before, I was now close to a full-on panic attack. The only solution was to turn around and chance driving back down the one-way road.

In backing to turn the car around, I heard a crunch! I had backed into a plastic barrier. With no other option, I jammed it into first gear and sped back toward the roundabout, hoping to avoid in-coming traffic (and the police). Just as I got to the roundabout, Courtney saw a sign to our right that said "Europcar." As we approached, there was no signage for returns, and it did not seem to be a drop-off location. I pulled past the building and got out to inspect my back bumper. Thankfully, there was no visible damage. As I got back in, a vehicle with a Europcar sticker pulled up to the dual set of traffic arms and both opened without hesitation. We thought, "Why not?" and followed him into the compound. He got out as if this had happened before explaining this was not the return area. I must have looked truly distressed because he quickly offered to show me where to go. He kindly drove us out of the compound and directly to the drop-off site.

I took a deep breath. I couldn't take much more. France was clearly telling us to go home. I got out and started unloading our luggage. The check-in guy thankfully spoke English and asked if we had any problems with the car. Knowing in my head that the side mirror had nothing more than a speck of paint missing, I said, nope everything was fine. He inspected the car carefully. He abruptly stopped while looking <u>under</u> the side mirror. I had not thought to look under the mirror after striking the medieval building. "There." He pointed; the side mirror blinker was cracked. He was very nice about it and said, "Don't worry. These things happen. I will send you an invoice." In my head, I groaned; Europcar, while being one of the most affordable rental agencies, was notorious for outrageous charges in cases like this. I imagined a bill for hundreds of euros and the hassle of trying to use the insurance provided by our credit card (we had declined the Europcar add-on). Skipping ahead in the story, a couple weeks later, I got a receipt for a seventy-five dollar charge for the damage which in the end seemed quite reasonable.

We dragged our luggage about a block to the airport and were relieved to find clear directions for the hotel. Unfortunately, it was at the end of a very long terminal. Running on empty, I greeted the front desk clerk in French. He quickly asked if I preferred to speak in French or English. I said, "English, if you don't mind. It has been a VERY long day." Check in was smooth. He invited us to eat dinner at the fancy restaurant in the hotel. Grubby and worn out, we declined and thought we'd pick up something fast in the terminal. The NH Toulouse Airport hotel was really quite nice and super convenient. We definitely wanted to get to the Air France desk but first had to deal with yet another stressor.

To get into France, all that was officially required was proof of vaccination and your word that you were not symptomatic. However, on arrival, we didn't have to show any proof, and no one asked if we were sick. To get back into the United States, you had to present a negative

COVID-19 test within twenty-four hours of departure. We had found a relatively easy way to take a proctored test remotely and had brought along the kits. While neither of us had symptoms, it was still anxiety provoking to consider what might be required if we didn't pass the test. We had read horror stories of asymptomatic Americans being quarantined for days while continuing to test positive. We connected to a remote proctor who watched us self-administer the tests. Fifteen minutes later, another proctor connected to read the results, sending them to us through the app. We each took our turn with the process, and other than the ubiquitous hassle of having to reset passwords, it was actually efficient and quite painless. To my frustration, the United States dropped all required testing to re-enter the country the week after we returned.

Before heading down to the Air France counter, Courtney wanted to wash her face. I turned on the television and the French news was the first channel to come up. I kid you not; the headline at the bottom of the screen read that the union of the French equivalent of our TSA was planning to strike... tomorrow. Delays and flight cancellations were predicted. This day just kept getting better! We walked to the Air France counter which of course was at the opposite end of the terminal. We passed a ton of quick food options... all closed. We felt lucky to find no line at Air France, and the clerk there was a friendly young woman with good English. When we explained our check-in predicament, she assured us she'd take care of it "tout suit" (right away). She worked and worked on it then called down a supervisor who stared at her screen with the same confused look. She apologized and explained that the system would only allow us to check-in the following morning. It was a super early flight. I asked her what time we should return to be safe. 4:00am was her answer.

We trudged back to the hotel to finalize our packing before a necessary early bedtime, but first, we needed food. It was late, and we hadn't eaten anything since noon. On our way back down the terminal, we looked for anything remotely quick (and French) to eat. We checked every side hallway. Nothing was open except, wait for it… a Starbucks. The two girls working the shop were pleasant and cheerful. They acted surprised to meet people from America. The sandwiches were actually quite good. Back in our room, we washed them down with the excellent Cahors. We were in our king-sized bed by 10pm, but at least for me, I was too wound from the day to easily get to sleep. Eventually, my eyelids started to droop, and France's very long goodbye finally ended. The 3am (9pm EST) alarm came way too early.

24

CULTURE SHOCK

S leeping fast, we were up on time and left the room a little before 4am arriving at the Air France desk at 4:05. We were the ninth party in line. No one was at the counters. Gradually, clerks meandered in at a leisurely pace. By the time they finally opened at 4:25, the line waiting to check-in was miles long. Once they opened, check-in went smoothly though we did not get adjoining seats. Given the strike, we felt lucky to make it through security but only after our backpacks screened negative for drugs. Once on the plane, we both caught some z's on the short flight to Charles de Gaulle.

We now had an eight-hour layover in Paris. Since the Métro system is so easy to use, we had seriously considered putting our hand luggage in an airport locker and going into town. With the security strike, we now thought that unwise. As we walked from the domestic to the international terminal, we caught a glance in the other direction. There, travelers in the security line, as far as the eye could see, were trying to come in from Paris. We were glad to already be inside the terminal, and our early morning departure, now, didn't seem so bad. We had to pass through customs which usually makes me tense, but the border guard hardly looked at our passports waving us through.

Stuck in the international terminal for eight hours wasn't as bad as it sounds. We snagged two very comfy seats. There was a ton of high-end shopping, and Courtney enjoyed window shopping (or "lèche-vitrine," one of my favorite French expressions meaning literally "to lick the windows"). I wrote while she shopped. I was pleased to see a number of well-known French bakeries and restaurants. Unfortunately, just like in America, the airport versions of these establishments didn't quite measure up to the real thing. Watching the day progress, it was clear the strike had many travelers running late. They would get off the shuttle and break into a sprint toward their gate. Despite the chaos, the crowded terminal was remarkably quiet with people considerately talking in nothing more than a low murmur. The overhead announcements chimed in periodically in an agreeable, sing-songy French.

When it finally came time to head to our gate for our flight to Atlanta, we walked to the end of a corridor to the very last gate. The ambiance was palpably different. Much louder, I could hear the details of almost every conversation around me. Many were loudly complaining about how rude the French were. When it came time to queue the line, there was a mad rush. Without any airline perks, we were in the last group, and not having much hand luggage to store overhead, we casually took our place near the back of the line. Finally making it to the front, a Delta clerk shook her head and informed us we did not have the correct sticker on our boarding pass. She gestured sharply, explaining we would have to visit the table outside the line. Studying our boarding passes, the staff at the table looked confused. The best we can figure is that the stickers indicated proof of a negative COVID-19 test. I suspect all who entered at CDG got stickers at check-in, but no one in Toulouse even asked if we had been tested. Since the plane was about to leave, they slapped stickers on our boarding passes, without asking for any results, and hurried us back to the line. Finally in our seats, we could relax and settle in for the long flight to Atlanta.

The flight was uneventful. As we approached Atlanta, I began to worry about customs. During our tour of Gascony, I had purchased six bottles of Armagnac (if you partake of an extensive free tasting, it is etiquette to buy at least one bottle). Knowing that the stated customs limit was a one-liter allowance of liquor per person, I was fully expecting to pay an excise tax on the overage I was attempting to bring home. On the distillery visits, I had not thought about keeping receipts for this purpose. I had some but not all of the receipts.

During our last week on the trip, I realized my mistake. I took inventory of which receipts I did have. I planned to pack one liter (actually 1.25 liters but who's counting?) without receipts in Courtney's bag. That way, she could declare she was within limits and pass through. I planned to pack the three+ liters for which I did have receipts in my bag. Praying that customs wouldn't confiscate them for their own enjoyment, I was hoping to pay a reasonable import fee and get them through. This left one bottle without a receipt. During the end of our trip, I decided to drink one and chose the Delord 1989 vintage. We sipped on it through the last week. As a side note, the bottles were all quite affordable on-site at the distilleries, but on our return, when I checked the going rate for each in America, they were all worth three to six times what I paid for them. Just my luck, the one we chose to drink before leaving was by far the most valuable bottle in the states!

Getting off the flight in the Atlanta, the international terminal was chaotic. People were running to catch connections. We were all funneled into a set of old school metal detectors where the instructions were not clearly posted, even in English. TSA officers were shouting about what went through the conveyor belt (bags) and what did not (belts, coins, keys). Not the typical process for security, it was confusing to us but even more so to arriving foreigners who didn't speak the language. No one seemed to be completing the process properly, which led to more shouting. We eventually passed through the exit and into a large customs hall. We got into the much shorter line for returning Americans.

We had not been given any declarations paperwork. We had a choice and picked out a lane with a friendly looking, heavy-set agent. Bored with his job, he rattled off the list of items he was monitoring: guns, knives, excessive sums of money, and finally, "Any alcohol?" I took a deep breath and spoke for us. "She has a liter of liquor in her suitcase, and I have... three liters in mine." I swallowed hard and tried to look at him with kind eyes. Eyebrows raised, he responded curiously, "Hmm, so where'd you go?" I answered, "France." He paused then smiled with a wink and said, "Pass on through." He didn't check for our COVID testing status either.

Now 9pm on the East Coast and up for twenty-four hours, we looked and felt like death warmed over. We both went to the bathroom to wash our faces and brush our teeth. Finding our gate was easy, but our plane was delayed. Exhausted, we sat down across from the crowded gate and were slapped full on with a brutal case of culture shock. To our left, there was a young woman with her midriff hanging out having a shouting match with her boyfriend on speaker phone. To our right, a group of frat boys were loudly bragging about how drunk they had been the night before. And, standing square in the middle of the hallway was a group of southern rednecks decked out in camouflage with their arms crossed, staring a challenge at anyone who dared to make eye contact. To top it off, a shrill, screeching voice never stopped on the intercom. "Davis and Miller parties to the podium! Jackson and Dobson report to the podium!" I had expected relief to be home, but instead, I leaned over to Courtney and whispered, "Can we go back?" After several more delays and then an eternity waiting for our luggage at the Raleigh airport, our Uber driver dropped us off at 1:45am (almost twenty-nine hours from when we woke). Working the next morning at 8am was a challenge, but I was able to sleepwalk through it, living on good memories.

25

JE PARLE UN PEU PLUS FRANÇAIS [I SPEAK A LITTLE MORE FRENCH]

It is difficult to sum up the trip mentioning just a few highlights; ce n'est pas possible! As you have seen, we squeezed absolutely everything we possibly could out of our three-week stay. We are firm believers that the best way to experience a place is on the ground. By this metric, we definitely succeeded. Crisscrossing wide swaths of the country, we saw a large cross section of France. In the end, we took 320,000 steps, biked 11 kilometers, canoed 16 km's, drove 1230 km's, rode the Metro 210 km's and the high speed (TGV) train 600 km's. We tried our very best to assimilate, following the rules to soak up as much culture as we could. We feel lucky to have had so many amazing experiences.

When thinking of Paris, many images flash in my mind: Unexpectedly running into our favorite French movie star the day after Courtney joked our trip wouldn't be complete without it. Cycling

Versailles on a beautiful day with the fountains running in full display. Flaneuring the little piece of heaven called the Coulée Verte. Finding the hidden speakeasy, "The Little Red Door," and enjoying its funky and convivial atmosphere. Dining experiences ranging from a five-star extravaganza to eating in the home of a welcoming and warm, every-day Parisian. And, of course, seeing the Eiffel Tower light show both from the water, and on our last night, from our picnic blanket on the Champ de Mars.

Abruptly shifting from frenetic and glitzy Paris to quiet and bucolic Gascony taught us to savor slow tourism. Contemplating Gascony, I first think of the beauty, the serenity, and the friendly welcome of Les Bruhasses (and its "table d'hôtes"). I see an image in my mind of dining with a castle view at sunset then wandering alone in the medieval fortification at dusk. Likewise, I recall exploring a stunning circular bastide by streetlight after yet another terrific meal of duck. And, of course, I have to include the multiple bucket list visits to the finest houses of Armagnac with unbelievable, personal tours led by the owners themselves.

Just when we thought it couldn't get better, we found ourselves in the Dordogne creating completely different but equally indelible memories: Wandering the ancient maze of tiny passageways in the town where time stood still, Sarlat-la Canéda. A stormy night leading to a gastronomic tour de force with our own personal gourmet chef. The one-of-a-kind, charming meal, eating at grandma's house, at La Borie Blanche. And finally, who could forget the personal tour of a hidden pre-historic cave deep within a dark and foreboding forest?

I realize that I tend to end all of my books this way, but I offer no apologies. The real joy of travel is in the people you meet. With our cultural observations and our series of extraordinary interactions, I hope I have disabused you of the widely held American stereotype of the French as cold and rude; they are anything but. When I ponder the people from this trip I will never forget, the list is long: Claudine, our Eatwith host, sharing her home in Montmartre with us, the multitude of waiters, shop keepers, sommeliers, and folks at markets who went out of their way to treat us with kindness—a special nod to the Madagascan woman and her daughter in Sarlat. Our Airbnb host and "bad boy" Herve apologizing for his English. Our friend Arnie, the humble west Texan turned internationally acclaimed chef happy to cook for two. Madame Borde, the delightful matron of the La Borie Blanche, who gave us the idea of sending North Carolina post cards. The 16,000-year-old woman. All of the wonderful hosts at the Armagnac houses—Laurence, the Delord family, M. Darzacq and his lovely granddaughter, and of course, the incomparable Josselin de Ravignan à Perquie. And last but definitely not least come Jean and Hélène who absolutely went out of their way to make our trip fantastic. The trip that was never going to happen happened, and it "happened" beyond our wildest dreams. As I finish writing, we have already made reservations to return to France in a mere six months. In 2014, we started with very little French, but now, I can say with confidence, "Nous parlon un peu plus français!"

ACKNOWLEDGMENTS

Self-publishing a book was certainly a learning experience for me. That being said, I didn't really "self" publish but instead relied on many others who were incredibly helpful. Thank you to my friend, colleague and fellow author, Dr. Damon Tweedy for his insights on both writing and publishing. Thanks also to my mother, Connie Kirchmann, a former English teacher, for the first, big picture edit, correcting sentence structure, tenses and my dreadful grammar. A professional editor proved invaluable. I am grateful for Susan Kellior (find her on FIVERR) for her precise edits transforming my prose into something much more polished. Thank you also to Susan for her enthusiastic response and encouragement which spurred me to follow through on this project. Thanks to my beta readers Sarah Tiegreen, Michelle Turner, Jane Silver, Grace Gregson and Jacob Oberman for their valuable time and constructive feedback. I am lucky to have an outstanding business team in Kelsey Pasley, Ty Kirchmann and David Pasley. Their feedback, creative marketing ideas, and data analysis made this book so much more than my initial conception. For book design and formatting, thank you to the talented and professional Jose Peplto Jr. (also on FIVERR). Of course, I must thank the wonderful people of France whose names are detailed throughout this book. Thank you for being so patient, warm and welcoming! And last but not least, I must thank my wife Courtney, the love of my life, for being my rock, my constant companion and soul mate. May we continue to have fantastic adventures together the rest of our lives.

Made in the USA
Las Vegas, NV
27 December 2023

83600521R00132